Master Adobe Acrobat Dc 2025

Expert Techniques to Manage Documents and
Streamline PDF Creation, Editing, and Automation

Dana J. Bailey

Table of content

Part One:

Introduction to Adobe Acrobat

Overview of Adobe Acrobat

Adobe Acrobat is a family of software applications and web services developed by Adobe Inc. that allows users to view, create, manipulate, print, and manage Portable Document Format (PDF) files.

PDF is a widely used file format for sharing documents, ensuring that the formatting and layout remain consistent across different devices and platforms. Below is an overview of the main components and features of Adobe Acrobat:

Adobe Acrobat Reader:

- **Functionality:** Acrobat Reader is a free application that allows users to view, print, and annotate PDF files.

Key features:

- **View PDFs:** Open and view PDF documents.
- **Print:** Print PDF files with control over settings.
- **Comment and markup:** Add comments, annotations, and markups to PDFs.

Adobe Acrobat Standard:

- **Functionality:** Acrobat Standard is a paid desktop software that includes additional features beyond the basic Reader.

Key Features:

- **Create PDFs:** Generate PDF files from various sources, including scanned documents and web pages.
- **Edit PDFs:** Modify text and images within PDF documents.
- **Combine files:** Merge multiple files into a single PDF document.
- **Export to other formats:** Convert PDFs to Microsoft Word, Excel, or PowerPoint formats.

Adobe Acrobat Pro:

- **Functionality:** Acrobat Pro is a more advanced version of Acrobat Standard, offering additional tools and capabilities.

Key features:

- **Advanced editing:** Includes more sophisticated editing features, such as the ability to add or edit multimedia elements.
- **Form creation and editing:** Create interactive forms and collect form data.
- Security Features: Apply password protection, encryption, and digital signatures to secure PDF documents.
- **Batch processing:** Perform actions on multiple PDFs simultaneously.

Adobe Document Cloud:

- **Functionality:** Adobe Document Cloud is a set of cloud services that integrates with Acrobat software.

Key features:

- **Cloud storage:** Store and access PDFs in the cloud for easy sharing and collaboration.
- **E-signatures:** Use Adobe Sign to electronically sign documents and collect signatures.
- **Mobile access:** Access and work on PDFs across devices, including smartphones and tablets.

Adobe Acrobat online services:

- **Functionality:** Adobe offers various online services that complement the desktop applications.

Key features:

- **PDF conversion:** Convert documents to PDF format online.
- **PDF compression:** Reduce the file size of PDFs for easier sharing.
- **PDF export:** Convert PDFs to other file formats online.

Adobe Acrobat has become an industry standard for working with PDF files, and its features cater to a wide range of users, from individuals needing basic PDF viewing to professionals requiring advanced document manipulation and collaboration capabilities.

Understanding Acrobat as a comprehensive PDF solution

Adobe Acrobat is often considered a comprehensive PDF solution due to its extensive set of features and tools that cater to a wide range of tasks associated with Portable Document Format (PDF) files. Acrobat provides a free and widely used PDF viewer, Acrobat Reader, allowing users to open, view, and interact with PDF documents. This basic functionality is essential for anyone who needs to access PDF files.

Acrobat Standard and Pro editions enable users to create PDF files from various sources, including Microsoft Office documents, scanned images, web pages, and more. This feature is crucial for generating PDFs from different file formats. On the other hand, Acrobat Pro allows users to edit text, images, and other elements within PDF documents. This includes tasks such as adding, deleting, or modifying content, which is valuable for making changes to existing PDF files.

Acrobat enables users to merge multiple files into a single PDF document. This feature is helpful when consolidating various documents or pages into one cohesive file. Acrobat Pro includes tools for creating interactive forms. Users can design forms, add fields for data input, and create buttons and actions, making it a powerful solution for form creation and data collection.

Some other adobe products are:

- **Security and protection:** Acrobat offers robust security options, including password protection, encryption, and the ability to apply digital signatures. This ensures that sensitive information in PDF documents is safeguarded.
- **Collaboration and review:** Acrobat provides tools for adding comments, annotations, and markups to PDFs. This facilitates collaboration and feedback during the review process.
- **Cloud integration:** Integration with Adobe Document Cloud allows users to store, access, and share PDFs in the cloud. This enhances collaboration, especially when working with others who may not have the software installed locally.
- **E-signatures:** Acrobat integrates with Adobe Sign, a service for electronic signatures. This feature enables users to sign documents electronically and collect signatures from others, streamlining the signing process.
- **Mobile accessibility:** Acrobat supports viewing and editing of PDFs across various devices, including desktops, laptops, tablets, and smartphones. This ensures flexibility and accessibility for users on the go.
- **Advanced processing:** Acrobat Pro allows for batch processing, enabling users to perform actions on multiple PDF files simultaneously. This is particularly useful for tasks such as applying consistent settings or making repetitive modifications.

Importance of PDFs in digital documents

PDFs (Portable Document Format) play a crucial role in the world of digital documents due to several important reasons. PDFs are designed to be platform-independent, meaning they can be viewed consistently on various devices and operating systems. This ensures that the formatting and layout of the document remain intact regardless of the device used to open it. PDFs preserve the original formatting, fonts, images, and layout of a document. This ensures that the document looks the same on any device, preventing issues related to different software or operating system versions.

PDFs support encryption and password protection, allowing users to secure their documents. This is particularly important for sensitive or confidential information, providing a level of security that is crucial in various professional and legal contexts. PDFs are typically read-only by default, preventing accidental or unauthorized modifications. This feature is valuable for maintaining the integrity of important documents and ensuring that the content remains unchanged. PDFs offer consistent print results across different printers and systems. This is vital for industries where printed documents need to maintain a standardized appearance, such as in legal documents, contracts, and official reports.

In addition, PDFs support efficient compression algorithms, allowing for smaller file sizes without significant loss of quality. This is advantageous for efficient storage, faster document transfer, and easier sharing over the internet. PDFs support interactive elements, such as forms and multimedia content. This makes them versatile for creating documents that require user input, interactive navigation, or embedded videos and links. PDF/A is a specialized version of PDF designed for digital preservation. It ensures that documents remain self-contained and can be reliably reproduced over time, making PDF a suitable format for long-term archiving of digital documents.

Some other key aspects of PDF in digital documents are highlighted below

- **Standardization and Compliance:** PDF is an International Organization for Standardization (ISO) standard (ISO 32000). This standardization contributes to the widespread adoption of PDFs and ensures consistency in how PDFs are created and interpreted across different software applications.
- **Cross-Application Compatibility:** PDFs can be created from a variety of applications and can be opened using numerous PDF viewers. This interoperability is crucial for users who work with diverse software tools and need a common format for sharing documents.
- **Digital Signatures:** PDFs support digital signatures, providing a secure and legally recognized way to sign documents electronically. This is essential in industries where signed agreements and contracts are a routine part of business transactions.

Acrobat versions and updates

Adobe Acrobat has a history of different versions and tracks. The current version is Adobe Acrobat DC, which is available in two tracks:

- Continuous
- Classic

The Continuous track provides new features, security mitigations, feature enhancements, and bug fixes through regular updates. On the other hand, the Classic track offers only major releases that need to be purchased.

Updates for Acrobat are free, and they are essential for security and improved functionality. The installation time for updates is only a few minutes, and they can be managed through the application's preferences. The support for older versions, such as Acrobat 2015, has ended. Adobe

Acrobat DC is available for Windows 7, Windows 8, and Windows 10, as well as for Mac OS X 10.9 or later

Overview of the latest features and improvements

The latest features and improvements in Adobe Acrobat include:

- **Navigate and select text freely across paragraphs:** Users can now navigate and select text across paragraphs using the cursor, making it easier to edit and manipulate text within documents.
- **Customize all tools:** This feature allows users to create custom tools for specific tasks, streamlining the editing process.
- **Multiple touchpoints for combining files:** Users can now combine files from multiple sources, making it easier to work with complex documents.
- **Edit PDFs from your iPhone:** Adobe Acrobat now allows users to edit PDFs directly from their iPhones, including changing text, formatting, editing lists, and adding, rotating, and resizing images.
- **Improved SharePoint integration:** Adobe Acrobat has improved its integration with SharePoint and OneDrive, providing time-saving PDF tools and a new Acrobat PDF web viewer.
- **Unified Fill & Sign tool for signers and senders:** This feature simplifies the process of filling and signing documents for both signers and senders.
- **Enhancements in new Acrobat:** The latest release of Acrobat includes various enhancements to improve the overall user experience.

These features and improvements aim to enhance the user experience and provide more efficient tools for working with PDF documents.

Getting Started

You need to first install the software before you can explore its basic features and understand how to work with PDF documents. Follow the step-by-step guide below to help you get started with Adobe Acrobat:

- **Installation:** If you don't have Adobe Acrobat installed on your computer, you can download it from the official Adobe website. Follow the installation instructions provided by the installer.
- **Launch Adobe Acrobat:** After installation, launch Adobe Acrobat from your desktop or start menu.
- **Explore the User Interface:** Familiarize yourself with the main components of the Adobe Acrobat user interface, including the toolbar, menu bar, and side panels. The toolbar contains various tools for tasks like viewing, editing, and commenting on PDFs.
- **Open a PDF file:** Click on "File" in the menu bar. Then select "Open" to open an existing PDF file. After that, navigate to the location of your PDF and click "Open."

- **Basic navigation:** Use the navigation tools to move around the PDF. Zoom in and out using the zoom tools or pinch gestures. Navigate between pages using the navigation arrows or page thumbnails.
- **Viewing options:** Experiment with different viewing options, like Single page, Continuous, or Two-page view. Use the "Read Mode" for a distraction-free reading experience.
- **Basic editing:** Acrobat allows basic editing of PDF content. Click on "Edit PDF" in the toolbar to add, edit, or delete text. Use the "Add Image" tool to insert images into the PDF.
- **Commenting and markup:** Explore the commenting tools for collaboration: Highlight text, add comments, and draw annotations. Use the comment panel to manage annotations.
- **Creating PDFs:** Adobe Acrobat allows you to create PDFs from various sources. Click on "File" > "Create" to generate a PDF from a file or scanner. Combine multiple files into a single PDF using the "Combine Files" option.
- **Form handling:** If you're working with forms, use the "Prepare Form" tool to create interactive forms. Fill out and save forms directly in Adobe Acrobat.
- **Security features:** Explore security options for protecting your PDFs. Use password protection and encryption. Apply digital signatures for document integrity.
- **Exporting and saving:** Click on "File" > "Save" to save your modifications. Export PDFs to other formats if needed.
- **Adobe document cloud:** Sign up for an Adobe ID to access cloud storage and sharing options. Explore Adobe Sign for electronic signatures.

Chapter two

Installing Adobe Acrobat

System requirements and installation steps

Check below for installation steps and the system requirements for Adobe Acrobat:

System Requirements:

Windows:

- **Operating system:** Windows 10 or Windows 11.
- **Processor:** 1.5 GHz or faster.
- **RAM:** 2 GB or more.
- **Hard disk space:** 4.5 GB of available hard-disk space.
- **Display:** 1024x768 screen resolution.
- **Internet connection:** Required for product activation, software updates, and access to online services.

Mac:

- Operating system: macOS X v10.14 or later.
- Processor: Multicore Intel processor.
- RAM: 2 GB or more.
- Hard disk space: 4.5 GB of available hard-disk space.
- Display: 1024x768 screen resolution.
- **Internet connection:** Required for product activation, software updates, and access to online services.

Installation steps:

Download:

- Visit the official Adobe website.
- Sign in with your Adobe ID or create a new one.
- Go to the "Products" section and find Adobe Acrobat.
- Click on "Download" and follow the prompts.

Run the Installer:

- Once the download is complete, run the installer.
- Follow the on-screen instructions to begin the installation process.

Choose installation options: During the installation, you may be prompted to choose installation options, such as language and destination folder. Adjust these settings according to your preferences.

Sign in or activate:

- After installation, launch Adobe Acrobat.
- Sign in with your Adobe ID if prompted.
- Activate the software using your product key or serial number.

Updates: Check for updates after installation to ensure that you have the latest features and security patches. In the software, go to "Help" > "Check for Updates."

Explore features: Familiarize yourself with the Adobe Acrobat interface and explore its features by opening a PDF document and trying out different tools.

Activation and licensing options

Adobe Acrobat uses a licensing system that involves activation to ensure that users have valid and authorized access to the software. There are different licensing options available, depending on your needs. Here's an overview of activation and licensing options in Adobe Acrobat:

Activation

Activation is the process of verifying the legitimacy of the software and ensuring that it is being used in accordance with the licensing agreement. When you install Adobe Acrobat on your computer, you typically need to activate it by signing in with your Adobe ID and providing the necessary credentials.

Licensing options

Adobe offers various licensing options to cater to different user needs, including individual users, businesses, and enterprises. Some of them are highlighted below:

Individual License (Single User):

- **Subscription (Adobe Creative Cloud):** Adobe Acrobat DC is often available as part of the Adobe Creative Cloud subscription. Users pay a monthly or annual fee for access to the latest version of the software, including updates and additional features. Activation is linked to the user's Adobe ID.
- **Perpetual License (Adobe Acrobat 2020):** Some users may choose to purchase a perpetual license for Adobe Acrobat 2020, where they pay a one-time fee for the software. Activation is typically linked to the user's Adobe ID, and the license remains valid for the purchased version.

Business and enterprise licensing:

Adobe offers licensing options for businesses and enterprises to manage multiple users efficiently as highlighted below:

- **Enterprise Term License Agreement (ETLA):** ETLA is a flexible licensing option for large organizations. It provides access to Adobe Acrobat and other Adobe products for a specific term, usually three years. It allows for centralized deployment and management.
- **Volume Licensing:** Adobe provides volume licensing options for businesses with multiple users. This allows organizations to purchase a specific number of licenses based on their needs.

License management

Adobe provides tools for managing licenses efficiently, especially for businesses with multiple users. This includes the Adobe Admin Console, where administrators can assign and reassign licenses, manage users, and monitor usage.

Adobe document cloud

Adobe Document Cloud is integrated with Adobe Acrobat, and it provides additional services such as cloud storage, electronic signatures (Adobe Sign), and collaboration features.

Deactivation

If you need to move your Adobe Acrobat license to another computer, you may need to deactivate it on the current device before activating it on the new one. Deactivation helps manage the number of concurrent activations based on your licensing agreement.

Updates

Users with subscription-based licenses, such as those through Adobe Creative Cloud, receive automatic updates as long as their subscription is active. Perpetual license users may need to check for updates manually.

Navigating the user interface

Adobe Acrobat's user interface is designed to be intuitive, providing easy access to a wide range of tools and features for working with PDF documents. Check below for some of the main elements of the Adobe Acrobat user interface and how to navigate it:

- **Menu bar:** At the top of the application window, you'll find the menu bar containing various menus such as File, Edit, View, Tools, Window, and Help. These menus offer access to a wide range of commands and options.
- **Toolbar:** The toolbar is located just below the menu bar and provides quick access to frequently used tools. The tools available on the toolbar may include options for viewing, editing, commenting, and more.
- **Tools pane:** On the right side of the application window, you'll find the Tools pane. It provides a comprehensive set of tools categorized for different tasks, such as View, Edit, Comment, Fill & Sign, and more. Click on a category to expand and access specific tools.

- **Navigation pane:** The navigation pane, typically on the left side, allows you to navigate through your document. It may include options for thumbnails, bookmarks, attachments, and more. Click on the icons in this pane to switch between different navigation views.
- **Document area:** The central part of the application window is the document area. This is where you view and interact with the content of your PDF document. Use the scroll bars or mouse wheel to navigate through pages.
- **Zoom controls:** Zoom controls are available in the toolbar and often in the bottom-right corner of the document area. Use these controls to zoom in or out of the document.
- **Page navigation:** Page navigation controls, usually located at the bottom of the document area, allow you to jump to specific pages, move to the next or previous page, or scroll continuously through the document.
- **Commenting and markup tools:** Access commenting and markup tools from the toolbar or the Tools pane. These tools enable you to add comments, annotations, highlights, and other markings to your PDF.
- **Search and find:** Use the search bar in the toolbar to find specific words or phrases within the document. The Find tool is often available in the Edit menu as well.
- **View modes:** Change the view mode of your document using options like Single Page, Continuous Scroll, Two-Page View, etc. These options are typically available in the toolbar or the View menu.
- **Task panes:** Task panes provide additional options and information related to specific tasks. For example, the Comment pane allows you to manage comments and annotations.
- **Status bar:** The status bar at the bottom of the application window displays information about the document, such as page number, zoom level, and document size.
- **Access additional features:** Explore menus like Edit, Tools, and View to access additional features, such as editing text and images, creating forms, and applying security settings.
- **Adobe sign integration:** If you are using Adobe Sign for electronic signatures, there may be integration points within the user interface for managing signing workflows.
- **Adobe document cloud integration:** Adobe Document Cloud features, such as cloud storage and sharing options, may have integration points accessible from the user interface.

Toolbars, panels, and menus

Adobe Acrobat, toolbars, panels, and menus are essential components of the user interface, providing access to a wide range of tools and features.

Toolbars:

- **Main toolbar:** Located just below the menu bar. It contains frequently used tools for basic actions such as zooming, navigating pages, and searching.
- **Secondary toolbars:** Depending on the task at hand (e.g., editing, commenting, form filling), secondary toolbars may appear dynamically, offering context-specific tools. Secondary toolbars provide quick access to tools related to the current operation.

Panels:

Tools pane: Located on the right side of the application window. Organized into categories such as View, Edit, Comment, Fill & Sign, and more. Each category expands to reveal specific tools related to the selected task.

- **Navigation pane:** Found on the left side of the application window. Contains different panels for navigating through the document, such as Pages, Bookmarks, and Attachments. Allows users to switch between different views to focus on thumbnails, bookmarks, etc.
- **Comment pane:** A panel that appears when working with comments and annotations. Allows users to view and manage comments, highlights, and other markups.
- **Properties pane:** Appears when editing text, images, or other document properties. Provides options for adjusting settings related to the selected object.

Menus:

- **Main menu bar:** Located at the top of the application window. It contains menus such as File, Edit, View, Tools, Window, and Help. Each menu includes a dropdown list of commands and options related to its category.
- **Contextual menus:** Right-clicking within the document or certain panels often opens contextual menus. These menus provide quick access to relevant commands based on the context of the user's actions.

Customization

- **Custom toolbars:** Users can customize toolbars by adding or removing tools based on their preferences. Right-click on the toolbar area and select "Customize Quick Tools" to make adjustments.
- **Workspaces:** Acrobat offers predefined workspaces (e.g., Print Production, Reading, Editing) to optimize the arrangement of panels and tools for specific tasks. Users can create and save their custom workspaces.

Accessibility:

- **Accessibility tools:** Adobe Acrobat provides accessibility features to assist users with disabilities. The Accessibility panel allows users to check and enhance the accessibility of PDF documents.

Additional Considerations:

- **Adobe sign integration:** Tools and panels related to Adobe Sign may appear when working with electronic signatures.
- **Adobe document cloud integration:** Options for cloud storage, sharing, and collaboration may be accessible through menus and panels.

- **Search and find:** Search tools are often available in the toolbar or as a panel to locate specific content within the document.

Customizing the workspace

Customizing the workspace in Adobe Acrobat allows you to tailor the interface to your preferences and work more efficiently. Here's a guide on how to customize the workspace in Adobe Acrobat:

- **Open Adobe Acrobat:** Launch Adobe Acrobat on your computer.
- **Access the tool center:** On the right side of the toolbar, you'll find the "Tools Center." Click on the "Tools" tab to access the Tool Center.
- **Customize the Tool Center:** In the Tool Center, you can customize the tools that are readily available. To do this, click on the gear icon (usually labeled "Customize") or right-click on the tool you want to customize. Here, you can add or remove tools from the toolbar.
- **Customize the Quick Tools:** You can also customize the Quick Tools section, which is a customizable toolbar located just below the menu bar. To customize Quick Tools, click on the "More Tools" icon (usually represented by three dots or a small triangle) and choose "Customize Quick Tools." Here, you can drag and drop tools to rearrange them or add/remove tools from the toolbar.
- **Adjust the Navigation pane:** The Navigation Pane is on the left side of the Acrobat window. You can customize it by clicking the small arrow icon to show or hide the pane. You can also choose what tabs are displayed (e.g., Pages, Bookmarks, Attachments) by clicking on the corresponding icons.
- **Customize the ribbon:** In some versions of Adobe Acrobat, you may have a ribbon-style toolbar at the top. If so, you can usually customize it by right-clicking on it and selecting "Customize the Ribbon" or a similar option. This allows you to add or remove tabs and commands.
- **Adjust preferences:** For more advanced customization options, go to "Edit" > "Preferences" (Windows) or "Acrobat" > "Preferences" (Mac). Here, you can tweak settings related to the overall appearance, behavior, and functionality of Adobe Acrobat.
- **Save custom workspace:** After making your customizations, you may want to save your workspace. Go to "View" > "Show/Hide" > "Toolbar Items" > "Save As New Toolbar." This allows you to save your customized workspace for future use.

Customizing preferences

Customizing preferences in Adobe Acrobat allows you to tailor the software to your specific needs and preferences. Follow the tips below to customize preferences in Adobe Acrobat:

- **Open Adobe Acrobat:** Launch Adobe Acrobat on your computer.
- **Access Preferences:** On Windows, go to "Edit" > "Preferences." On Mac, go to "Acrobat" > "Preferences."

- **Explore Categories:** Preferences are organized into various categories on the left side of the Preferences dialog box. These categories include General, Page Display, Accessibility, and more.
- **Adjust General Preferences:** Under the "General" category, you can set preferences related to the general behavior of Adobe Acrobat. This may include options for default view settings, language, and startup options.
- **Configure Page Display preferences:** Navigate to the "Page Display" category to customize settings related to how pages are displayed, such as default zoom levels, page layout, and smooth scrolling.
- **Modify Accessibility preferences:** If accessibility is a concern, you can customize settings under the "Accessibility" category. This includes options for high-contrast colors, text-to-speech, and other accessibility features.
- **Adjust Commenting preferences:** If you frequently work with comments and annotations, explore the "Commenting" category to customize preferences related to comment appearance, authoring, and handling.
- **Explore other categories:** Depending on your needs, explore other categories like "Security," "Documents," or "Updater" to customize preferences related to document security, handling, and software updates.
- **Apply changes:** After making your desired changes, click the "OK" or "Apply" button to save your preferences. In some versions of Acrobat, you may need to restart the application for the changes to take effect.
- **Reset to defaults:** If you ever want to revert to the default preferences, most versions of Adobe Acrobat provide a "Restore Defaults" or "Reset All" button within the Preferences dialog box.

Adjusting settings for a personalized experience

Creating a personalized experience in Adobe Acrobat involves adjusting various settings to suit your preferences and workflow. The tips below will guide you.

- **Open Adobe Acrobat:** Launch Adobe Acrobat on your computer.
- **Access Preferences:** On Windows, go to "Edit" > "Preferences." On Mac, go to "Acrobat" > "Preferences."
- **General preferences:** In the "General" category, you can customize settings for the overall behavior of Adobe Acrobat. This may include options for default view settings, language, and startup options. For example, you can set your preferred units for measurements, change the default zoom level, or adjust the language settings.
- **Page Display Preferences:** Navigate to the "Page Display" category to customize settings related to how pages are displayed. Adjust default zoom levels, page layout, and enable or disable features like smooth scrolling. These settings can significantly impact your reading experience.
- **Commenting Preferences:** If you frequently work with comments and annotations, explore the "Commenting" category to customize preferences related to comment appearance,

authoring, and handling. Adjust settings to match your preferred style for markups and comments.

- **Toolbar customization:** Customize the toolbar by right-clicking on the toolbar area. You can add or remove tools to create a toolbar that suits your workflow. This is especially useful if there are specific tools you use frequently.
- **Quick tools:** Customize the Quick Tools section, located below the menu bar. Click on the "More Tools" icon and choose "Customize Quick Tools." Here, you can add or remove tools from the toolbar, allowing you to access your most-used tools easily.
- **Navigation pane:** Adjust the Navigation Pane on the left side of the Acrobat window. You can choose what tabs are displayed (e.g., Pages, Bookmarks, Attachments) based on your preferences. Click on the small arrow icon to show or hide the pane.
- **Preferences for document handling:** Explore categories like "Documents" to customize preferences related to document handling. You may find options to control how documents open, save, and close.
- **Security preferences:** If security is a concern, navigate to the "Security" category to customize settings related to document security. Adjust settings to enhance the security of your documents based on your needs.
- **Updater preferences:** In the "Updater" category, customize settings related to software updates. You can choose how often Adobe Acrobat checks for updates and whether to install them automatically.
- **Apply Changes:** After making your desired changes in the Preferences dialog box, click "OK" or "Apply" to save your preferences. In some cases, you may need to restart Adobe Acrobat for the changes to take effect.

Setting default document view preferences

It allows you to customize how your documents are displayed by default when you open them. The steps below will guide you:

Open Adobe Acrobat: Launch Adobe Acrobat on your computer.

Access Preferences: On Windows, go to "Edit" > "Preferences." On Mac, go to "Acrobat" > "Preferences."

Navigate to the "Page Display" Category: In the Preferences dialog box, find and click on the "Page Display" category on the left sidebar.

Adjust Default settings: Within the "Page Display" category, you'll find various options related to how documents are displayed.

Adjust the following settings based on your preferences:

- Default Layout: Choose between Single Page, Continuous, or Two-Up display.
- Zoom: Set the default zoom level for opening documents.
- Page Transitions: If you want to use page transition effects, you can set them here.

Other settings include:

- **Additional Preferences:** Depending on your preferences, you might also want to explore other options in the "Page Display" category, such as:
- **Show large images:** Choose whether to display large images or down sample them for faster rendering.
- **Smooth text:** Enable or disable smooth text for a sharper display.
- **Apply changes:** After adjusting the settings to your liking, click "OK" or "Apply" to save the changes.
- **Test the changes:** Open a PDF document to test whether the changes you made to the default view preferences are applied.

Creating PDFs

The methods below can guide you when creating PDFs:

Using Adobe Acrobat:

- Open Adobe Acrobat on your computer.
- Click on "File" in the menu bar.
- Select "Create" and then choose "PDF from File" or "PDF from Scanner" based on your source.
- Follow the prompts to select the file or scanner settings.

Using Microsoft Office applications:

- Open the document you want to convert to PDF in Microsoft Word, Excel, or PowerPoint.
- Click on "File" and choose "Save As" or "Export."
- Select "PDF" as the format and adjust settings if necessary.
- Click "Save."

Using the Print option:

- Open the document you want to convert.
- Click on "File" and choose "Print."
- In the print dialog, select the Adobe PDF printer from the list of printers.
- Click "Print" and follow the prompts to save the PDF.

Combining multiple files into a PDF:

- Open Adobe Acrobat.
- Click on "File" and choose "Create" > "Combine Files into a Single PDF."
- Add the files you want to combine and arrange them if needed.
- Click "Combine" and save the new PDF.

Using Drag-and-Drop:

- Open Adobe Acrobat.
- Locate the file(s) you want to convert to PDF in File Explorer (Windows) or Finder (Mac).
- Drag and drop the file(s) onto the Adobe Acrobat window.
- Adjust settings if necessary and save the PDF.

Creating PDFs from web pages:

- Open the webpage you want to convert to PDF.
- Click on "File" and choose "Print."
- In the print dialog, select the Adobe PDF printer.
- Click "Print" and save the PDF.

Chapter 3

Creating PDFs from different file formats
Converting Word, Excel, and other file types to PDF

Follow the steps below:

Converting Word to PDF
Microsoft Word (Online):

- Open the Word document.
- Click on "File" in the top left corner.
- Select "Save As" > "Download as PDF."
- Save the PDF file to your desired location.

Microsoft Word (Desktop):

- Open the Word document.
- Click on "File" in the top left corner.
- Select "Save As."
- Choose the location where you want to save the PDF.
- In the "Save as type" dropdown, select PDF.
- Click "Save."

Converting Excel to PDF
Microsoft Excel (Online):

- Open the Excel spreadsheet.
- Click on "File" in the top left corner.
- Select "Save As" > "Download as PDF."
- Save the PDF file to your desired location.

Microsoft Excel (Desktop):

- Open the Excel spreadsheet.
- Click on "File" in the top left corner.
- Select "Save As."
- Choose the location where you want to save the PDF.
- In the "Save as type" dropdown, select PDF.
- Click "Save."

Converting Other File Types to PDF

Using Online Converters:

- There are various online converters available. Choose a reputable one like SmallPDF, Zamzar, or Adobe's online PDF converter.
- Upload your file to the online converter.
- Select the desired output format as PDF.
- Click on the conversion button.
- Download the converted PDF file.

Using Software Applications

- If you have software like Adobe Acrobat, you can use it to convert various file types to PDF.
- Open the software.
- Click on "File" > "Create" > "PDF from File" or a similar option.
- Select the file you want to convert.
- Click "Convert" or "Create."

Using Print Option (For Various File Types)

- Open the file you want to convert (e.g., a webpage, image, or text file).
- Click on "File" > "Print" (or use the shortcut Ctrl + P on Windows or Command + P on Mac).
- In the print dialog, choose "Print to PDF" or a similar option.
- Click "Print" or "Save."

Mobile Devices

- On mobile devices, you can use apps like Microsoft Word, Excel, or Google Docs/Sheets to open your files.
- Once opened, look for the option to export or save the document as a PDF.
- Save the PDF file to your device.

Using the Print to PDF option

The "Print to PDF" option is a convenient feature available on many operating systems that allows you to convert various types of files into PDF format. The steps below will guide you on how to do this successfully.

Using "Print to PDF" on Windows:

- **Open the File:** Open the file you want to convert to PDF using an application like Microsoft Word, Excel, a web browser, or any other software.
- **Select Print:** Click on "File" in the top left corner of the application. Choose "Print" or use the keyboard shortcut (Ctrl + P).
- **Choose Printer:** In the Print dialog box, under "Printer," select "Microsoft Print to PDF" or a similar option.
- **Configure Print settings:** Adjust print settings as needed, such as page range, orientation, or size.
- **Print:** Click "Print." Choose the location where you want to save the PDF file. Next, enter a file name and click "Save."

Using "Print to PDF" on Mac:

- **Open the File:** Open the file you want to convert to PDF using an application like Microsoft Word, Excel, a web browser, or any other software.
- **Select Print:** Click on "File" in the top menu. Choose "Print" or use the keyboard shortcut (Command + P).
- **Configure Print Settings:** In the Print dialog box, locate the "PDF" button in the lower-left corner.
- **Choose "Save as PDF":** Click on the "PDF" button, and from the dropdown menu, select "Save as PDF."
- **Set Save Location:** Choose the location where you want to save the PDF file.
- **Enter file name:** Enter a file name for the PDF.
- **Save:** Click "Save."

Benefits of "Print to PDF" Option

- **Universal availability:** The "Print to PDF" option is available in almost every application that supports printing, making it a universal and versatile choice.
- **Consistent quality:** The resulting PDF maintains the original document's layout, formatting, and quality.
- **Customizable Settings:** Users can often customize print settings, such as page orientation, size, and other print options before converting to PDF.
- **Integration with existing software:** Since this option is integrated into the standard print dialog, users don't need to install additional software.

Combining multiple files into a single PDF

Follow the steps below:

Method 1: Using Online Tools

Several online tools allow you to merge multiple files into a single PDF. One popular option is SmallPDF.

- Visit SmallPDF: Go to the SmallPDF website (https://smallpdf.com/merge-pdf).
- Upload Files: Click on the "Choose Files" button and select the files you want to merge. You can also drag and drop files into the designated area.
- Arrange Files: Arrange the files in the desired order if the tool allows you to do so.
- Merge PDF: Click on the "Merge PDF" button.
- Download Merged PDF: Once the merging process is complete, download the merged PDF file to your computer.

Method 2: Using Adobe Acrobat DC

If you have Adobe Acrobat DC, you can combine files into a PDF directly.

- **Open Adobe Acrobat DC:** Launch Adobe Acrobat DC on your computer.
- **Click on "Tools":** In the upper left corner, click on "Tools."
- **Select "Combine Files":** Under "Combine Files," click on "Combine."
- **Add Files:** Click on the "Add Files" button and select the files you want to merge. You can also drag and drop files into the window.
- **Combine:** Click on the "Combine" button.
- **Save Merged PDF:** Save the merged PDF by clicking on "File" > "Save" or "File" > "Save As."

Method 3: Using Preview on Mac

If you're using a Mac, you can use the Preview application to merge PDFs.

- **Open preview:** Open the Preview application on your Mac.
- **Open the first PDF:** Click on "File" > "Open" and select the first PDF file.
- **View thumbnails:** Click on "View" > "Thumbnails" to show thumbnail views of the pages.
- **Drag additional PDFs:** Drag and drop additional PDF files into the thumbnail view.
- **Export as PDF:** Click on "File" > "Export as PDF."
- **Save merged PDF:** Save the merged PDF file to your desired location.

Merging PDFs with the Combine Files tool

Combining multiple files into a single PDF is a common task, especially when you want to create a comprehensive document or presentation. Here's how you can do it using different methods:

Method 1: Using online tools

Several online tools allow you to merge multiple files into a single PDF. One popular option is SmallPDF.

- **Visit SmallPDF:** Go to the SmallPDF website (https://smallpdf.com/merge-pdf).
- **Upload files:** Click on the "Choose Files" button and select the files you want to merge. You can also drag and drop files into the designated area.
- **Merge PDF:** Click on the "Merge PDF" button.
- **Download merged PDF:** Once the merging process is complete, download the merged PDF file to your computer.

Method 2: Using Adobe Acrobat DC

If you have Adobe Acrobat DC, you can combine files into a PDF directly.

- **Open Adobe Acrobat DC:** Launch Adobe Acrobat DC on your computer.
- **Click on "Tools":** In the upper left corner, click on "Tools."
- **Select "Combine Files":** Under "Combine Files," click on "Combine."
- **Add files:** Click on the "Add Files" button and select the files you want to merge. You can also drag and drop files into the window.
- **Combine:** Click on the "Combine" button.
- **Save merged PDF:** Save the merged PDF by clicking on "File" > "Save" or "File" > "Save As."

Method 3: Using Preview on Mac

If you are using a Mac, you can use the Preview application to merge PDFs.

- **Open preview:** Open the Preview application on your Mac.
- **Open the first PDF:** Click on "File" > "Open" and select the first PDF file.
- **View Thumbnails:** Click on "View" > "Thumbnails" to show thumbnail views of the pages.
- **Drag additional PDFs:** Drag and drop additional PDF files into the thumbnail view.
- **Export as PDF:** Click on "File" > "Export as PDF."
- **Save merged PDF:** Save the merged PDF file to your desired location.

Rearranging and organizing pages

The steps below will guide you:

- **Open PDF in Adobe Acrobat DC:** Launch Adobe Acrobat DC and open the PDF document that you want to edit.
- **Access page thumbnails:** Click on the "View" menu in the top toolbar and select "Show/Hide" > "Navigation Panes" > "Page Thumbnails." This will open the Page Thumbnails pane on the left side.
- **View thumbnails:** In the Page Thumbnails pane, you will see a thumbnail view of all pages in the document.
- **Select and drag pages:** Select the page or pages you want to move by clicking on the corresponding thumbnail(s). Drag the selected page(s) to the desired position in the thumbnail view.
- **Drop pages in new position:** Release the mouse button to drop the selected page(s) in the new position.
- **Save changes:** After rearranging the pages, click on "File" > "Save" or "File" > "Save As" to save the changes to the PDF document.

Scanning documents into PDF format

Scanning documents into PDF format is a common task that allows you to create digital copies of physical documents. The process involves using a scanner or a multifunction printer with scanning capabilities. Follow the guideline below:

Scanning Documents into PDF

- **Place the document:** Put the document you want to scan face down on the scanner bed. Ensure that the document is aligned properly. Turn on the Scanner: Power on the scanner or multifunction printer.
- **Open scanner software:** Open the scanning software on your computer. This software is often provided by the scanner manufacturer.
- **Select scan settings:** Choose the scanning settings such as color mode (color, grayscale, or black and white), resolution, and file format. For scanning to PDF, select PDF as the output format.
- **Preview:** Some scanning software allows you to preview the scanned document before saving it. Previewing can help you make adjustments to the scan area.
- **Scan the document:** Click the "Scan" or "Start" button to begin scanning the document.
- **Save as PDF:** After the scan is complete, you will be prompted to save the scanned document. Choose the PDF format as the file type.
- **Specify file name and location:** Enter a file name for the PDF document and choose the location where you want to save it.
- **Finish and review:** Complete the scanning process, and review the saved PDF document to ensure it meets your requirements.

- **Using a Multifunction Printer (MFP):** If you are using a multifunction printer with scanning capabilities:
- **Load the document:** Load the document into the feeder or on the scanner bed.
- **Access scanner functions:** Navigate to the scanning functions on the printer's control panel.
- **Select PDF as Output Format:** Choose PDF as the output format.
- **Adjust Settings:** Adjust scanning settings such as resolution and color mode.
- **Start Scanning:** Start the scanning process using the printer's control panel.
- **Save as PDF:** Once the scan is complete, you may be prompted to save the scanned document. Choose the PDF format and specify the file name and location.
- **Review the PDF:** Check the saved PDF document to ensure it is accurate and legible.

Scanning settings and best practices

In Adobe Acrobat, you can utilize various scanning settings and best practices to optimize the scanning process for your documents. Check below for details:

Scanning Settings in Adobe Acrobat:

- **Open Adobe Acrobat:** Launch Adobe Acrobat on your computer.
- **Select "Scan" from Home Screen:** Click on "Tools" in the upper-left corner, then select "Create PDF" and choose "Scanner."
- **Choose scanner:** Select your scanner from the list of available devices.
- **Configure scan settings:** Adobe Acrobat provides options to configure your scan settings. Adjust the following settings as needed:
- **Scanner:** Choose your scanner from the list.
- **Mode:** Select color, grayscale, or black and white.
- **Resolution:** Set the DPI (dots per inch) for the scan. Higher DPI offers better quality but results in larger file sizes.
- **Page size:** Choose the appropriate page size for your document.
- **Orientation:** Set the orientation to portrait or landscape.
- **Preview the scan:** Adobe Acrobat allows you to preview the scan before finalizing it. This helps you ensure that the document is correctly positioned on the scanner bed.
- **Additional settings:** Depending on your scanner and Adobe Acrobat version, you may have additional settings like color correction, despeckle, or background removal.
- **Scan:** Click the "Scan" button to start the scanning process.
- **Review and save:** After the scan is complete, review the document. If satisfied, click on "File" > "Save" or "File" > "Save As" to save the PDF.

Best Practices:

- **Choose the right resolution:** For standard documents, a resolution of 300 DPI is usually sufficient. Higher resolutions are beneficial for detailed images or high-quality scans.

- **Consider file size:** Higher resolutions and color depths result in larger file sizes. Be mindful of your storage and sharing requirements.
- **Preview before scanning:** Always preview the scan to ensure proper document placement. Adjust the scan area if necessary.
- **OCR for text recognition:** If you need searchable and editable text, enable OCR. This is especially helpful for documents you want to search or edit later.
- **Organize scanned pages:** If scanning multiple pages, Adobe Acrobat allows you to organize, rotate, and delete pages before saving the PDF.
- **Save settings as preset:** If you have specific scanning settings, save them as a preset for future use.

OCR (Optical Character Recognition) for scanned text

- Open Adobe Acrobat DC.
- Open the scanned document you want to perform OCR on.
- Go to "Tools" in the upper left corner.
- In the "Tools" pane, choose "Enhance Scans."
- Click on "Recognize Text" in the Enhance Scans panel.
- Select "In This File" if you want to recognize text only in the current document.
- Choose "All Pages" if you want to apply OCR to all pages.
- Select the language of the text in your document.
- Click on the "Recognize Text" button.
- After OCR is complete, save your document.
- Please note that Adobe Acrobat XI is an older version, and it's recommended to use the latest version if possible.
- Open Adobe Acrobat XI.
- Open the scanned document you want to perform OCR on.
- Go to "File" > "Save As" > "Microsoft Word" or "Other Formats."
- In the "Save As" dialog, choose the file type "Word Document (*.docx)" or "RTF."
- Before saving, click on the "Settings" button.
- In the Settings dialog, check the option "Run OCR."
- Choose the correct language for your document.
- Click "OK" to close the Settings dialog.
- Click "Save" to initiate OCR and save the document.

Editing and Modifying PDFs
Adding and editing Text:

- Select the "Edit PDF" tool from the right pane.
- Click on the text you want to edit.

- Add new text or modify existing text.

Adding images:

- Click on "Edit PDF" and select the "Add Image" tool.
- Choose the image file and place it on the PDF.

Adding links:

- Click on the "Link" tool in the "Edit PDF" pane.
- Drag to draw a rectangle where you want the link.
- Specify the link destination.

Adding or removing pages:

- Click on "Organize Pages" in the right pane.
- To add a page, click "Insert" > "Page from File" or "Blank Page."
- To remove a page, select it and press the delete key.

Splitting or merging PDFs

- Use the "Organize Pages" tool.
- To split, select the page, right-click, and choose "Extract."
- To merge, drag and drop PDF files into the "Organize Pages" pane.

Adding comments and annotations

- Use the "Comment" tool from the right pane.
- Add text comments, highlights, sticky notes, etc.

Redacting sensitive information:

- Use the "Redact" tool in the "Protect" pane.
- Select text or area to redact and apply.

Password protection:

- Go to "File" > "Protect Using Password."
- Choose whether to restrict editing, printing, or both.

9. OCR (Optical Character Recognition):

- Use the "Enhance Scans" tool.
- Click on "Recognize Text" to make scanned text searchable.

Flattening layers:

- If your PDF has layers, go to "View" > "Show/Hide" > "Navigation Panes" > "Layers."

- Right-click on a layer and choose "Flatten Layers."

Form editing:

- Use the "Prepare Form" tool.
- Click on form fields to edit or add new fields.

Headers and footers:

- Go to "File" > "Print" > "Header and Footer."
- Add or edit headers and footers as needed.

Page numbering:

- Go to "File" > "Print" > "Page Numbers."
- Add or customize page numbers.

Editing document properties:

- Go to "File" > "Properties."
- Update document properties like title, author, etc.

Save and export:

- After making changes, save the document.
- To export to different formats, go to "File" > "Export."

Chapter four

Adding, deleting, and rearranging pages

Inserting Pages:

- Open Adobe Acrobat DC.
- Open the PDF document where you want to insert pages.
- Click on "Tools" in the upper left corner.
- Choose "Organize Pages" from the Tools Center.
- Click on the "Insert" button in the Organize Pages toolbar.
- Choose whether you want to insert pages from another PDF file, a scanner, or a file.
- Specify the range of pages or select the file you want to insert.
- Confirm your choices and save the modified PDF.

Extracting Pages

- Open Adobe Acrobat DC.
- Open the PDF document from which you want to extract pages.
- Click on "Tools" in the upper left corner.

- Choose "Organize Pages" from the Tools Center.
- Choose the pages or page range you want to extract.
- Right-click on the selected pages.
- Choose "Extract" from the context menu.
- Specify a name for the new PDF file containing the extracted pages.
- Save the file.

Rotating pages

- Open Adobe Acrobat DC.
- Open the PDF document where you want to rotate pages.
- Click on "Tools" in the upper left corner.
- Choose "Organize Pages" from the Tools Center.
- Choose the pages or page range you want to rotate.
- Right-click on the selected pages.
- Choose "Rotate" from the context menu.
- Select the direction of rotation (clockwise or counterclockwise).
- Click "OK" to apply the rotation.

Managing page thumbnails

- Open Adobe Acrobat DC.
- Open the PDF document you want to work with.
- Click on "View" in the top menu.
- Select "Show/Hide" and choose "Navigation Panes" > "Pages."
- This will open the Pages pane on the left side of the screen, displaying page thumbnails.

Rearranging Pages:

- Open the Pages pane.
- Click on a page thumbnail and drag it to the desired position.
- Release the mouse button to drop the page in its new position.
- Open the Pages pane as described earlier.
- Right-click on the thumbnail of the page(s) you want to delete.
- Select "Delete" from the context menu.
- Confirm the deletion when prompted.

Extracting pages

- Open the Pages pane.
- Right-click on the thumbnail of the page(s) you want to extract.
- Select "Extract Pages" from the context menu.
- Specify the page range and choose where to save the extracted pages.
- Open the Pages pane.
- Right-click on the thumbnail of the page(s) you want to rotate.
- Select "Rotate Pages" from the context menu.
- Choose the desired rotation direction (clockwise or counterclockwise).
- Click "OK" to apply the rotation.

Changing Page Layout

- Open the Pages pane.
- Right-click on the thumbnail of the page(s) you want to adjust.
- Select "Page Properties" from the context menu.
- In the Page Properties dialog, you can adjust the width, height, and orientation.

Editing text and images

Editing Text:

- Open Adobe Acrobat DC.
- Open the PDF document you want to edit.
- Click on "Tools" in the upper left corner.
- Choose "Edit PDF" from the Tools Center.
- Click on the text you want to edit.
- Make changes to the text using the available tools in the Edit toolbar.
- Use the formatting options in the toolbar to change font, size, color, etc.
- Select the "Add Text" tool to add new text to the document.
- After editing, save your document.

Editing images:

- Open Adobe Acrobat DC.
- Open the PDF document containing the image you want to edit.
- Click on "Tools" and choose "Edit PDF."
- Click on the image you want to edit.
- Right-click on the image and choose "Edit Image."
- Resize, move, or replace the image using the editing handles.
- To replace the image, right-click, choose "Replace Image," and select a new image file.
- After editing, save your document.

Using the Edit Text and Edit Image tools

Edit text:

- Launch Adobe Acrobat DC.
- Open the PDF file you want to edit.
- Click on "Tools" in the upper left corner.
- Choose "Edit PDF" from the Tools Center.
- Click on the text you want to edit.
- If the document has editable text, you can modify it directly.
- Make changes using the text editing tools in the toolbar.
- Adjust font size, color, and other formatting options as needed.
- Select the "Add Text" tool to insert new text.
- After making edits, save your document.

Edit image:

- Open Adobe Acrobat DC.
- Open the PDF file containing the image you want to edit.
- Access the Edit Image tool:
- Click on "Tools" and choose "Edit PDF."
- Click on the image you want to modify.
- Right-click on the image and choose "Edit Image."
- Resize, move, or replace the image using the editing handles.
- If you choose "Edit Using," you can open the image in an external image editor.
- To replace the image, right-click, choose "Replace Image," and select a new image file.
- After editing, save your document.

Changing fonts, colors, and sizes

- Launch Adobe Acrobat DC.
- Open the PDF file you want to edit.
- Click on "Tools" in the upper left corner.
- Choose "Edit PDF" from the Tools Center.
- Click on the text you want to modify.
- After selecting the text, you should see the Text Properties toolbar at the top of the screen. If it's not visible, you can find it by clicking on "Format" in the Edit toolbar.
- Use the "Font" dropdown menu in the Text Properties toolbar to select a different font.
- Use the "Font Size" dropdown or manually enter a font size to adjust the text size.
- Click on the "Fill Color" icon in the Text Properties toolbar to change the text color.
- Select a new color from the color picker.
- After making edits, save your document.

Inserting links and bookmarks

Inserting Links:

- Launch Adobe Acrobat DC.
- Open the PDF file you want to add links to.
- Click on "Tools" in the upper left corner.
- Choose "Edit PDF" from the Tools Center.
- Click on the "Link" tool in the toolbar.
- Click and drag to draw a rectangle around the area you want to link.
- In the Create Link dialog, choose the link action. This can be a web link, a link to another page in the document, or a link to an external file.
- Depending on the link type, you may need to provide additional information such as the URL, page number, or file path.
- After creating links, save your document.

Inserting Bookmarks:

- Launch Adobe Acrobat DC.
- Open the PDF file you want to add bookmarks to.
- Click on "View" in the top menu.
- Choose "Show/Hide" > "Navigation Panes" > "Bookmarks."
- Navigate to the page you want to bookmark.
- Right-click on the page thumbnail in the Pages pane or Document view.
- Choose "New Bookmark."
- Double-click on the new bookmark and enter a descriptive name.
- Drag and drop bookmarks to arrange them in a hierarchical structure if needed.
- To create nested bookmarks, drag a bookmark slightly to the right under another bookmark.
- After creating bookmarks, save your document.

Creating hyperlinks and cross-references

Creating hyperlinks:

- Launch Adobe Acrobat DC.
- Open the PDF file you want to add hyperlinks to.
- Click on "Tools" in the upper left corner.
- Choose "Edit PDF" from the Tools Center.
- Click on the "Link" tool in the toolbar.
- Click and drag to draw a rectangle around the area you want to link.
- In the Create Link dialog, choose the link action. This can be a web link, a link to another page in the document, or a link to an external file.
- Depending on the link type, you may need to provide additional information such as the URL, page number, or file path.

- After creating hyperlinks, save your document.

Creating Cross-References:

- Launch Adobe Acrobat DC.
- Open the PDF file you want to add cross-references to.
- Click on "Tools" in the upper left corner.
- Choose "Edit PDF" from the Tools Center.
- Click on the "Link" tool in the toolbar.
- Click and drag to draw a rectangle around the area you want to link.
- In the Create Link dialog, choose "Custom Link."
- In the "Link Properties" dialog, choose "Go to a page view."
- Specify the destination page and view.
- After creating cross-references, save your document.

Adding and organizing bookmarks for navigation

Adding bookmarks:

- Launch Adobe Acrobat DC.
- Open the PDF file you want to add bookmarks to.
- Click on "View" in the top menu.
- Choose "Show/Hide" > "Navigation Panes" > "Bookmarks."
- Navigate to the page you want to bookmark.
- Right-click on the page thumbnail in the Pages pane or Document view.
- Choose "New Bookmark."
- Double-click on the new bookmark and enter a descriptive name.
- Repeat steps 3-4 for each section or page you want to bookmark.

Organizing bookmarks:

- Open the Bookmarks pane as described above.
- To organize bookmarks, you can drag and drop them to arrange them in a hierarchical structure.
- Indent a bookmark under another to create a nested structure.
- Right-click on a bookmark and choose "Properties" to rename it.
- Right-click on a bookmark and choose "Delete" to remove it.

Setting Destinations for Bookmarks

- Go to the page or section you want to link to.
- Right-click on the page thumbnail or a selected area.
- Choose "New Bookmark" to create a bookmark linked to the current view.

Annotations and Comments
Adding Annotations:

Launch Adobe Acrobat DC.

Open the PDF file you want to annotate.

Click on "Tools" in the upper left corner.

Choose "Comment" from the Tools Center.

Click on the tool you want to use from the Comment toolbar.

Common tools include:

- Text Comment: Add a text note.
- Highlight Text: Highlight selected text.
- Drawing Markups: Add shapes, lines, and freeform drawings.
- Stamp Tool: Add predefined or custom stamps.
- Note Tool: Add a pop-up note.

Apply the annotation:

- Click on the document where you want to add the annotation.
- For text comments, simply start typing in the note.
- Right-click on the annotation to access formatting options.
- Adjust colors, styles, and other properties as needed.
- After adding annotations, save your document.

Reviewing comments

- Open the Comment pane on the right side of the screen.
- Click on a comment in the Comment List to jump to its location in the document.
- Reply to comments, resolve them, or mark them as done.

Chapter 5

Highlighting text and adding comments
Using the Highlight, Underline, and Strikethrough tools

Highlighting text:

- Launch Adobe Acrobat DC.
- Open the PDF file you want to annotate.
- Click on "Tools" in the upper left corner.
- Choose "Comment" from the Tools Center.
- Click on the "Highlight Text" tool in the Comment toolbar.
- Click and drag to select the text you want to highlight.

Underlining text

- Launch Adobe Acrobat DC.
- Open the PDF file you want to annotate.
- Click on "Tools" in the upper left corner.
- Choose "Comment" from the Tools Center.
- Click on the "Underline Text" tool in the Comment toolbar.
- Click and drag to select the text you want to underline.

Strikethrough Text:

- Launch Adobe Acrobat DC.
- Open the PDF file you want to annotate.
- Click on "Tools" in the upper left corner.
- Choose "Comment" from the Tools Center.
- Click on the "Strikethrough Text" tool in the Comment toolbar.
- Click and drag to select the text you want to strikethrough.

Adding sticky notes and text comments
Adding Sticky Notes:

- Launch Adobe Acrobat DC.
- Open the PDF file you want to annotate.
- Click on "Tools" in the upper left corner.
- Choose "Comment" from the Tools Center.
- Click on the "Sticky Note" tool in the Comment toolbar.
- Click on the location in the document where you want to add the sticky note.
- Type your comments into the sticky note.
- Click and drag to move the sticky note.

- Drag the corners to resize it.

Adding Text Comments

- Launch Adobe Acrobat DC.
- Open the PDF file you want to annotate.
- Click on "Tools" in the upper left corner.
- Choose "Comment" from the Tools Center.
- Click on the "Text Box" tool in the Comment toolbar.
- Click on the location in the document where you want to add the text box.
- Type your comments into the text box.
- Click and drag to move the text box.
- Drag the corners to resize it.

Drawing shapes and adding markups

Drawing Shapes:

- Launch Adobe Acrobat DC.
- Open the PDF file you want to annotate.
- Click on "Tools" in the upper left corner.
- Choose "Comment" from the Tools Center.
- Click on the "Drawing Markups" tool in the Comment toolbar.
- Click on the desired shape tool, such as the rectangle, ellipse, or line tool.
- Click and drag on the location in the document where you want to draw the shape.
- After drawing the shape, you can adjust its size and position by clicking and dragging its handles.

Adding markups

- Launch Adobe Acrobat DC.
- Open the PDF file you want to annotate.
- Click on "Tools" in the upper left corner.
- Choose "Comment" from the Tools Center.
- Click on the "Drawing Markups" tool in the Comment toolbar.
- Select a markup tool, such as the arrow, line, or pencil tool.
- Click and drag on the location in the document where you want to add the markup.
- After adding the markup, you can adjust its size and position by clicking and dragging its handles.
- Drawing tools, shapes, and lines

Drawing Tools

- Launch Adobe Acrobat DC.
- Open the PDF file you want to annotate.
- Click on "Tools" in the upper left corner.
- Choose "Comment" from the Tools Center.
- Click on the "Comment" toolbar, then click on "Drawing Markups."
- In the "Drawing Markups" toolbar, you'll find various drawing tools such as the Pencil, Line, Arrow, Rectangle, Ellipse, and Polygon tools.

Drawing shapes:

- Select the Rectangle or Ellipse Tool:
- Click on the "Rectangle" or "Ellipse" tool in the Drawing Markups toolbar.
- Click and drag to draw the rectangle or ellipse on the location in the document.
- Click on the "Polygon" tool in the Drawing Markups toolbar.
- Click to set each corner of the polygon. Double-click to finish drawing.
- Select the Line or Arrow Tool:
- Click on the "Line" or "Arrow" tool in the Drawing Markups toolbar.
- Click and drag to draw the line or arrow on the location in the document.

Drawing Freeform:

- Click on the "Pencil" tool in the Drawing Markups toolbar.
- Click and drag to draw freeform lines on the location in the document.
- Right-click on a drawn shape or line to access options for adjusting colors, styles, and other properties.
- Open the Comment pane to review and manage all annotations in your document.
- Customize the appearance and behavior of annotation tools through the "Comment" toolbar.

Using the Drawing Markup panel

- Open the PDF document in Adobe Acrobat.
- Look for the "Comment" or "Markup" tools. These are typically located in a toolbar on the right side of the screen.
- Depending on your version, you may find tools like "Pencil," "Line," "Arrow," or "Shapes" within the Comment or Markup toolbar.
- Select the desired drawing or markup tool, and then use your mouse or touch input to draw or mark up the document.
- After drawing, you may be able to adjust properties such as color, line thickness, or fill. Look for options in the toolbar or properties panel.
- Save your changes to the PDF document.

Using comments for collaboration

Adding Comments:

- Open the PDF document you want to collaborate on using Adobe Acrobat.
- Look for the "Comment" or "Markup" tools in the toolbar on the right side of the screen.

Next is to choose a comment tool based on the type of feedback you want to provide. Common tools include:

- Sticky Note: Adds a text comment.
- Highlight Text: Highlights selected text.
- Strikethrough Text: Crosses out selected text.
- Underline Text: Underlines selected text.
- Drawing Tools: Allows you to draw shapes or freeform annotations.
- Click on the location in the document where you want to add the comment, and enter your feedback.

Reviewing comments:

- Use the Comments panel to navigate through the comments in the document. You can typically find this panel on the right side of the screen.
- If someone has left a comment, you can reply to it by right-clicking on the comment and selecting "Reply."

Collaborative features

- Save the document with the comments, and share the PDF file with others. Comments are usually saved within the document.
- Some versions of Adobe Acrobat include a review tracker that allows you to see a summary of all comments and their status.
- If you are using Adobe Acrobat Pro DC and have access to Adobe Document Cloud, you may be able to collaborate in real time with others. This allows multiple users to view and comment on a PDF simultaneously.

Finalizing comments:

- In some cases, you may want to summarize comments or mark them as resolved to track progress.
- Export comments to a separate file if needed.
- Save the PDF document to retain all the comments and annotations.

Tracking changes and resolving comments

Tracking changes:

- Use the Comment tools to add various types of comments, such as Sticky Notes, Highlights, Strikethroughs, and more. Collaborators can see these comments when they open the PDF.
- Open the Comments panel on the right side of the screen. This panel displays a list of all comments in the document.
- Use the Comments panel to navigate through comments. Clicking on a comment in the panel will jump to that comment in the document.

Resolving comments:

- Right-click on a comment and select "Reply" to respond to a comment. This can be useful for communication and clarification.
- If a comment has been addressed and no longer needs attention, you may want to mark it as resolved. Right-click on the comment in the Comments panel and select "Resolve."
- If there are numerous comments, you may want to summarize them. Some versions of Adobe Acrobat allow you to generate a summary of all comments.

Collaborative features:

- Save the PDF with comments included and share the document with others. The comments are saved within the document, allowing collaborators to see and respond to them.
- If you're using Adobe Acrobat Pro DC and have access to Adobe Document Cloud, you may be able to collaborate in real time. Multiple users can view and comment on the PDF simultaneously.

Finalizing changes:

- After resolving comments, save the PDF document to retain all the comments and annotations.
- If needed, you can export comments to a separate file for documentation or further review.

Exporting and importing comments

Exporting Comments:

- Open the PDF document in Adobe Acrobat.
- Open the Comments panel on the right side of the screen. This panel displays a list of all comments in the document.
- In the Comments panel, look for an option to export comments. This option is typically available in the options menu of the Comments panel.

You can now select the desired format for exporting comments and some of the common formats include:

- **XFDF (XML Forms Data Format):** A standard format for representing form data and annotations in a PDF.
- **FDF (Forms Data Format):** Similar to XFDF, FDF is another format for representing form data and annotations.

Afte selecting the format, choose a location on your computer to save the exported comments file.

Importing comments:

- Open the PDF document in Adobe Acrobat.
- Open the Comments panel on the right side of the screen.
- Look for an option to import comments in the Comments panel. This option is usually available in the options menu.
- Browse to the location where you saved the exported comments file and select it.
- After importing, review the Comments panel to ensure that the comments have been successfully imported.

Form creation and editing

Creating forms:

- Open the PDF document you want to turn into a form in Adobe Acrobat.
- Ensure that the document is ready for form creation. For example, if you're converting a non-interactive PDF, make sure the text and elements are in place.
- In Adobe Acrobat DC, go to "Tools" > "Prepare Form." This will open the Form Editing mode.
- Acrobat may attempt to recognize form fields automatically. Review the auto-generated fields, and make adjustments if needed.
- Use the form editing toolbar to add different types of form fields, such as text fields, checkboxes, radio buttons, and dropdown lists.
- After adding a form field, right-click on it and select "Properties" to adjust its properties, such as name, appearance, and validation.
- Define the tab order for navigating through the form fields. Go to "More" > "Show Tab Numbers" and adjust the tab order as needed.
- Save the form and test it to ensure that all form fields work as expected.

Editing forms:

- Open the PDF document containing the form in Adobe Acrobat.
- If you need to make changes to existing form fields or add new ones, go to "Tools" > "Prepare Form" to enter Form Editing mode.
- Click on the form field you want to edit. You can move, resize, or delete existing fields. Right-click on a field and choose "Properties" to adjust its settings.

- Use the form editing toolbar to add new form fields if necessary.
- Customize the properties of form fields by right-clicking on a field and selecting "Properties."
- Change the appearance of form elements, such as fonts and colors, as needed.
- Save your changes and test the form to ensure that the modifications are working as intended.
- Save the PDF document after making changes to retain the edited form.

Distributing forms:

- If you want to keep the original form intact, save a copy of the edited PDF.
- Share the PDF form with others. Users can fill out the form electronically and submit it.

CHAPTER 6

Creating interactive forms

Form fields, buttons, and text boxes

Adding form fields:

- Open the PDF document in Adobe Acrobat.
- Go to "Tools" > "Prepare Form" to enter Form Editing mode.

You can now use the form editing toolbar to add different types of form fields, such as:

- **Text field:** Allows users to enter text.
- **Check box:** Users can check or uncheck the box.
- **Radio button:** Users can choose one option from a group.
- **Combo box:** A drop-down menu for users to select from.
- **List box:** A list for users to select from.

Place and customize form fields

- Click and drag to place form fields on the document. Right-click on a field and choose "Properties" to customize its appearance and behavior.
- Define the tab order by going to "More" > "Show Tab Numbers" and adjusting the tab order.

Adding buttons:

- Enter Form Editing mode as described above.
- Use the form editing toolbar to add a "Button" form field.
- Right-click on the button and select "Properties." Customize the button appearance, actions, and other properties.
- Buttons can trigger various actions, such as opening a web link, playing a sound, or submitting the form. Configure these actions in the button properties.
- Open the PDF document in Adobe Acrobat.
- Use the "Add Text" tool in the toolbar to add a text box.
- Click and drag to create a text box. Adjust the size and position as needed.
- Right-click on the text box and choose "Properties" to customize the appearance and behavior of the text box.

Designing user-friendly forms

Follow the tips below:

- **Clear and simple layout:** Keep the layout clean and organized. Avoid clutter and ensure there is ample white space. Group related form fields together and use clear headings or labels.
- **Consistent design:** Maintain a consistent design throughout the form. Use a uniform font, color scheme, and styling for a cohesive look.
- **Intuitive navigation:** Set a logical tab order for form fields so that users can navigate through the form easily using the keyboard. Use clear labels and visual cues to guide users on how to fill out the form.
- **Use descriptive labels:** Clearly label each form field with descriptive text. Avoid jargon and use language that your users will understand.
- **Provide instructions:** Include clear and concise instructions at the beginning of the form or next to specific fields. Help users understand how to fill out the form correctly.
- **Utilize form fields appropriately:** Choose the right type of form field for the information you are collecting (text fields, checkboxes, radio buttons, etc.). Set default values when appropriate to reduce user input.
- **Error handling:** Implement validation checks to provide instant feedback if users enter information incorrectly. Clearly communicate any errors and provide instructions on how to correct them.
- **Interactive elements:** If using buttons or other interactive elements, ensure they are appropriately labeled and provide clear feedback when clicked. Consider using tooltips to provide additional information.
- **Accessibility considerations:** Ensure your form is accessible to users with disabilities. Use accessible fonts, provide alternative text for images, and ensure proper color contrast.
- **Testing:** Test the form extensively before distributing it. Check the form's functionality, readability, and overall user experience. Consider seeking feedback from potential users to identify any usability issues.
- **Save and resume functionality:** If applicable, consider adding a "Save and Resume" feature that allows users to save their progress and return to the form later.
- **PDF security:** If the form contains sensitive information, use PDF security features to protect the data and limit access.
- **Responsive design:** If users will be accessing the form on various devices, ensure the form design is responsive and works well on different screen sizes.
- **Document properties:** Set document properties, including metadata, to provide additional information about the form.
- **Instructions for submission:** Clearly state how users should submit the completed form, whether it's through email, an online portal, or another method.

Adding form fields and buttons
Adding form fields:

- Open the PDF document in Adobe Acrobat.
- Go to "Tools" > "Prepare Form" to enter Form Editing mode.

In the form editing toolbar, choose the type of form field you want to add. Common types include:

- **Text field:** For users to enter text.
- **Check box:** For users to check or uncheck.
- **Radio button:** For selecting one option from a group.
- **Combo box:** A dropdown menu for selecting from a list.
- **List box:** A list for selecting multiple options.

Place form field

- Click on the location in the document where you want to add the form field. Adjust the size and position as needed.
- Right-click on the form field and select "Properties" to customize its appearance, behavior, and other properties. Set options such as the field name, default value, and formatting.
- Define the tab order by going to "More" > "Show Tab Numbers" and adjusting the tab order.

Text fields, checkboxes, radio buttons, and dropdowns

Text fields:

- Open the PDF document in Adobe Acrobat.
- Go to "Tools" > "Prepare Form" to enter Form Editing mode.
- In the form editing toolbar, select the "Text Field" tool.
- Click on the location in the document where you want to add the text field. Adjust the size and position as needed.
- Right-click on the text field and select "Properties" to customize its appearance, behavior, and other properties.

Checkboxes:

- Enter Form Editing mode as described above.
- In the form editing toolbar, select the "Checkbox" tool.
- Click on the location in the document where you want to add the checkbox. Adjust the size and position as needed.
- Right-click on the checkbox and select "Properties" to customize its appearance, behavior, and other properties.

Radio buttons:

- Enter Form Editing mode as described above.
- In the form editing toolbar, select the "Radio Button" tool.
- Click on the location in the document where you want to add the radio button. Adjust the size and position as needed.

- Radio buttons work in groups. To create a group, create multiple radio buttons in close proximity. They will automatically become part of the same group.
- Right-click on a radio button and select "Properties" to customize its appearance, behavior, and other properties.

Dropdowns:

- Enter Form Editing mode as described above.
- In the form editing toolbar, select the "Dropdown" tool.
- Click on the location in the document where you want to add the dropdown. Adjust the size and position as needed.
- Right-click on the dropdown and select "Properties" to customize its appearance, behavior, and other properties.
- In the "Options" tab of the properties, define the list of options that will appear in the dropdown.

Customizing form field properties

- Open the PDF document in Adobe Acrobat.
- Go to "Tools" > "Prepare Form" to enter Form Editing mode.
- In the form editing toolbar, select the "Text Field" tool.
- Click on the location in the document where you want to add the text field.
- Right-click on the text field and select "Properties."
- In the General tab, you can set the field name, alignment, and maximum length.
- In the Format tab, you can specify the format of the text, such as numbers, dates, or custom patterns.
- Explore other tabs like Options and Actions to set additional properties and actions for the text field.

Customizing checkbox properties

- Enter Form Editing mode as described above.
- In the form editing toolbar, select the "Checkbox" tool.
- Click on the location in the document where you want to add the checkbox.
- Right-click on the checkbox and select "Properties."
- In the General tab, you can set the field name, export value, and appearance options.
- Explore other tabs like Options and Actions to set additional properties and actions for the checkbox.

Customizing radio button properties:

- Enter Form Editing mode as described above.
- In the form editing toolbar, select the "Radio Button" tool.
- Click on the location in the document where you want to add the radio button.
- Right-click on the radio button and select "Properties."
- In the General tab, you can set the field name, export value, and appearance options.
- Explore other tabs like Options and Actions to set additional properties and actions for the radio button.

Customizing dropdown properties

- Enter Form Editing mode as described above.
- In the form editing toolbar, select the "Dropdown" tool.
- Click on the location in the document where you want to add the dropdown.
- Right-click on the dropdown and select "Properties."
- In the General tab, you can set the field name and other general options.
- Go to the Options tab to define the list of options that will appear in the dropdown.
- Explore other tabs like Actions to set additional properties and actions for the dropdown.

Collecting form responses

- Open the PDF document you want to turn into a fillable form.
- Click on "Tools" in the upper left corner.
- Select "Prepare Form."
- Acrobat will automatically detect potential form fields. Review and edit them as needed.
- To add a new form field, click on the "Add a Text Field" or other form field type from the toolbar.
- Right-click on a form field and select "Properties" to configure settings such as the field name, appearance, and validation.
- Save the PDF document after adding all the necessary form fields.

Collecting Form Responses:

- Share the PDF form with your audience. This could be through email, a website, or any other distribution method.
- Recipients can open the PDF form using Adobe Acrobat Reader (or any PDF reader that supports form filling) and fill in the required information.
- Responses are automatically stored within the PDF file. When you open the PDF, go to the "Tools" menu and select "Forms" > "More Form Options" > "Manage Form Data" > "Export Data."
- Choose the format in which you want to export the form data (e.g., CSV or Excel).

- Save the exported data file to your computer and review the collected responses using a spreadsheet application.

Form distribution methods

- **Email distribution:** You can attach the PDF form to an email and send it directly to the intended recipients. Adobe Acrobat supports the creation of mailto links within the PDF, making it easy for users to submit the form via email.
- **Shared Network Location:** Save the PDF form on a shared network location, and provide the link to users. This method is useful for internal forms within an organization.
- **Online platforms:** Use online platforms or cloud services to host the PDF form, and share the link. Services like Dropbox, Google Drive, or SharePoint can be used for this purpose.
- **Embedding in websites:** Embed the form on a website or intranet. Users can access the form directly from the web page, fill it out, and submit it.
- **Adobe sign** If you need to collect digital signatures along with form responses, you can use Adobe Sign. This service allows you to send forms for e-signature, and it integrates with Adobe Acrobat.
- **Form distribution via CD/DVD:** Burn the PDF form onto a CD or DVD and distribute physical copies. This method is less common in the digital age but may be useful in specific situations.
- **Integration with Online Survey platforms:** Export the form to an online survey platform like Adobe FormsCentral (Note: Adobe FormsCentral has been discontinued, and alternative platforms can be used).
- **QR codes:** Generate a QR code linked to the form and include it on printed materials. Users can scan the QR code with their mobile devices to access and fill out the form.
- **Intranet or document management systems:** If your organization uses an intranet or document management system, you can upload the PDF form to these systems, making it easily accessible to employees.

Analyzing and exporting form data
Analyzing form data:

- Open the PDF form in Adobe Acrobat.
- Click on the "Tools" tab in the upper left corner of the screen.
- In the "Forms" pane, click on "More Form Options" and then select "Manage Form Data."
- In the "Manage Form Data" dialog box, choose the option "Export Data." This opens the "Export Data As" dialog box.
- Select the format in which you want to export the data. Common formats include "XML Forms Data (.xfdf)," "CSV (Comma Delimited) (.csv)," or "Excel Workbook (*.xlsx)."

- Choose a location on your computer to save the exported file, provide a file name, and click "Save."

If you choose to export data as a CSV or Excel file, you can further analyze the data in a spreadsheet program like Microsoft Excel or Google Sheets as described below:

- **Open the exported file:** Locate and open the exported file using your preferred spreadsheet application.
- **Review and analyze data:** Once the data is imported into the spreadsheet, you can analyze and manipulate it as needed. This may include sorting, filtering, and creating charts or graphs.
- **Save and share the analysis:** After analyzing the data, you can save the spreadsheet file and share it with others or use it for reporting purposes.

Basic security features

Password protection:

- Set a password to control who can open the PDF document.
- Set a password to restrict editing, printing, and other actions.

How to Set Passwords:

- Go to "File" > "Properties" > "Security" tab.
- Choose password options under "Password Security."

Certificate-based Security:

- Use digital certificates to encrypt and sign PDFs for enhanced security.
- Go to "Tools" > "Protect" > "Encrypt" > "Encrypt with Certificate."

Encryption:

- Encrypt PDF documents to protect their contents.
- Go to "File" > "Properties" > "Security" tab.
- Choose encryption options under "Password Security."

Digital signatures:

- Sign PDF documents with a digital signature for authentication and integrity.
- Go to "Tools" > "Protect" > "More Sign & Certify" > "Sign Document."

Redaction:

- Permanently remove sensitive information from a PDF using redaction tools.
- Go to "Tools" > "Protection" > "Mark for Redaction."

Document restrictions:

- Apply restrictions to control what users can do with the document (e.g., printing, copying text).
- Go to "File" > "Properties" > "Security" tab.
- Choose permissions options under "Password Security."

Secure viewing mode:

- Enable a secure viewing mode that limits certain actions, enhancing overall document security.
- Go to "Edit" > "Preferences" > "Security (Enhanced)" > "Enable Enhanced Security."

Automatic updates:

- Ensure that you are using the latest version of Adobe Acrobat to benefit from security updates and patches.
- Go to "Help" > "Check for Updates."

Protected view:

- Open documents in a protected view to mitigate potential security risks.
- Go to "File" > "Properties" > "Security" tab.
- Check the "Open in Protected View" option.

JavaScript security:

- Manage JavaScript settings to control the execution of potentially unsafe scripts.

CHAPTER 7

Setting password protection

The password creation and security considerations below will guide you:

- **Use strong passwords:** Create strong passwords that are difficult to guess. Use a combination of uppercase and lowercase letters, numbers, and special characters.
- **Differentiate open and permissions passwords:** If using both an open password (to control who can open the document) and a permissions password (to restrict actions like editing or printing), ensure they are distinct and offer different levels of security.
- **Avoid common words and phrases:** Do not use easily guessable passwords such as common words, phrases, or easily accessible personal information.
- **Consider certificate-based security:** For higher security, consider using digital certificates for encryption and authentication rather than relying solely on passwords.
- **Regularly update passwords:** Change passwords periodically to enhance security. Avoid using the same passwords for an extended period.
- **Apply encryption:** Encrypt the document using a strong algorithm. Adobe Acrobat supports AES encryption, which is considered highly secure.
- **Protect against unauthorized access:** Use passwords to prevent unauthorized access to sensitive PDF content, especially if the document contains confidential or personal information.

- **Specify document permissions:** When setting a permissions password, clearly define the actions that users are allowed or restricted to perform (e.g., printing, editing).
- **Be mindful of sharing passwords:** Only share passwords with authorized individuals. Avoid sharing passwords through insecure channels.
- **Consider document redaction:** Use redaction tools to permanently remove sensitive information from the document before applying security measures. This ensures that even if the document is accessed, certain information remains confidential.
- **Protect metadata:** Remove any metadata or hidden information that might contain sensitive details before applying password protection.
- **Educate users:** Educate users on the importance of password security and the potential risks associated with weak or shared passwords.
- **Backup passwords securely:** If you need to store passwords for document access or permissions, ensure that these are securely stored and not easily accessible to unauthorized individuals.
- **Update software regularly:** Keep Adobe Acrobat up to date to benefit from security updates and patches that address vulnerabilities.
- **Test aecurity measures:** Before finalizing security measures, test the document to ensure that the passwords work as intended and that the specified permissions are applied.

Removing password protection

To remove password protection from a PDF document in Adobe Acrobat, you need the password that was used to secure the document. If you have the correct password, follow these steps:

- Open the password-protected PDF file in Adobe Acrobat.
- When prompted, enter the password to open the document.
- Once the document is open, go to "File" in the top menu.
- Select "Properties."
- In the Properties dialog box, go to the "Security" tab.
- Under the "Security Method" drop-down menu, select "No Security."
- Click "OK" to apply the changes.
- Save the document by clicking "File" and then "Save" or "Save As."

Removing Permissions Password (to change security settings)

If the PDF is also protected with a permissions password (to restrict actions like printing or editing), follow these additional steps:

- Open the password-protected PDF file in Adobe Acrobat.
- Enter the permissions password when prompted.
- Once the document is open, go to "File" in the top menu.
- Select "Properties."
- In the Properties dialog box, go to the "Security" tab.

- Under the "Password Security" section, click on "Change Settings."
- Enter the permissions password again when prompted.
- In the Security Settings dialog box, set the security method to "No Security."
- Click "OK" to apply the changes.
- Save the document by clicking "File" and then "Save" or "Save As."

Redacting sensitive information

Redacting sensitive information in Adobe Acrobat involves permanently removing or obscuring confidential content from a PDF document. Follow the step-by-step instructions below on how to redact sensitive information:

Applying redaction:

- Launch Adobe Acrobat and open the PDF file that contains the sensitive information.
- Go to the "Redaction" Tool
- Click on the "Tools" pane on the right side of the screen.
- Under the "Protect & Standardize" section, choose "Redact."
- Select Text to Redact
- In the redaction toolbar, click on the "Mark for Redaction" tool.
- Highlight the text or area you want to redact.
- Mark Content for Redaction
- A red box will appear around the selected content. Right-click and choose "Mark for Redaction" from the context menu.
- Review and Confirm Redaction
- Review the redaction marks. If satisfied, go to the "Apply Redactions" tool in the redaction toolbar.

Redaction tools and techniques

Mark for redaction:

Use the "Mark for Redaction" tool to select and mark specific text or images for redaction.

Steps:

- Click on the "Tools" pane on the right side of the screen.
- Under "Protect & Standardize," select "Redact."
- Choose the "Mark for Redaction" tool.

- Highlight the text or area you want to redact.
- Right-click and select "Mark for Redaction."

Search and redact:

The "Search and Redact" tool allows you to find and redact all instances of a specific term or phrase throughout the document.

Steps:

- Click on the "Tools" pane.
- Under "Protect & Standardize," select "Redact."
- Choose the "Search and Redact" tool.
- Enter the search term and click "Search and Redact."

Apply redactions:

After marking content for redaction, use the "Apply Redactions" tool to permanently remove the selected information.

Steps:

- In the redaction toolbar, select the "Apply Redactions" tool.
- Confirm that you want to apply the redactions.

Examine document:

The "Examine Document" feature helps you review the document for hidden information and metadata before sharing the redacted version.

Steps:

- In the redaction toolbar, choose "Examine Document."

Redaction properties:

Adjust redaction properties to customize the appearance of redaction marks, such as color and overlay text.

Steps:

- In the redaction toolbar, click on "Properties."

Redaction code set:

Define a set of codes for specific types of redactions, providing a standardized way to categorize and track redactions. In the redaction toolbar, choose "Redaction Code Set."

Redaction tool options

Configure various redaction tool options, such as enabling or disabling overlays, changing the color of redaction marks, or setting default properties. In the redaction toolbar, click on the drop-down arrow next to the redaction tool.

Remove hidden information

Use the "Remove Hidden Information" tool to check for and remove any metadata or hidden content in the document. Go to "File" > "Properties" > "Security" tab > "Remove Hidden Information."

Reviewing redacted content

Reviewing redacted content ensures that sensitive information has been properly obscured or removed from the document. Follow the steps below to review redacted content:

- Open the PDF document that has undergone the redaction process in Adobe Acrobat.
- Look for visible redaction marks on the document. Redaction marks typically appear as colored boxes or other shapes that indicate the areas where content has been marked for removal.
- Select the "Hand Tool" from the toolbar to navigate through the document. This allows you to click and drag to move around the PDF, making it easier to inspect redacted areas.
- Use the zoom tools to zoom in and out of the document, especially in areas where redactions have been applied. This helps you closely examine the content and confirm that sensitive information is properly obscured.
- If an overlay text was added during the redaction process (e.g., to indicate the reason for redaction), ensure that it is visible and accurately conveys the intended information.
- Manually review each redacted area to ensure that the information within those regions is no longer visible. Pay close attention to text, images, or any other content that might have been redacted.
- Open the "Content" panel in Adobe Acrobat to view the document's structure. This can help identify any remaining elements that may need attention. Click on "View" > "Show/Hide" > "Navigation Panes" > "Content."

Search for hidden text or metadata: Run a search to check for any hidden text or metadata that might not have been properly redacted. Click on the "Tools" pane. Under "Protect & Standardize," select "Redact." Choose the "Examine Document" tool.

Ensure proper save: After reviewing and confirming the redactions, save the document. Saving ensures that the redacted content is permanently removed, and the changes are applied to the PDF.

Compare with original document: If available, compare the redacted document with the original (unredacted) version to confirm that the intended content removal has been successfully executed.

Certifying and signing PDFs

Certifying a PDF:

- Open the PDF file that you want to certify in Adobe Acrobat.
- Click on the "Tools" pane on the right side of the screen.
- Under the "Tools" pane, select "Protect & Standardize."
- Choose "Certify with Visible Signature" or "Certify Without Visible Signature"
- Select the "Certify with Visible Signature" option if you want to add a visible signature to the document. Choose "Certify Without Visible Signature" if you prefer an invisible certification.
- Follow the on-screen prompts to set certification preferences, including specifying permitted actions and creating a reason for certification.
- If you haven't created a digital ID, Adobe Acrobat will prompt you to do so. Follow the steps to create a digital ID, which is necessary for certification.
- If you chose a visible signature, position the signature field on the document as desired.
- Follow the prompts to complete the certification process, including saving the document.

Adding a Digital Signature to a PDF

- Open the PDF file you want to sign in Adobe Acrobat.
- Click on the "Tools" pane on the right side of the screen.
- Under the "Tools" pane, select "Protect & Standardize."
- Choose "Sign & Certify" > "Place Signature"
- Select "Sign & Certify" and then choose "Place Signature."
- If you haven't created a digital ID, Adobe Acrobat will prompt you to do so. Alternatively, you can use an existing digital ID.

Position and resize the signature field

- Position the signature field on the document where you want your signature to appear. You can also resize the field as needed.
- Click on the signature field to sign the document. Adobe Acrobat will prompt you to enter your digital ID password to complete the signing process.
- After signing, save the document to apply the digital signature.

Verifying signatures

- Open the signed PDF document in Adobe Acrobat.
- Right-click on the signature field and select "Properties" to view details about the signature, including the signer's identity and timestamp.
- In the "Signature" panel, you can check the signature status. A valid signature indicates that the document has not been altered since it was signed.

Creating digital signatures

- Launch Adobe Acrobat on your computer.

- Click on the "Edit" menu in the top menu bar.
- Select "Preferences" from the dropdown menu.
- In the Preferences window, choose "Security" on the left-hand side.
- Under the "Security" settings, click on the "Advanced Preferences" button.
- In the Advanced Security Settings window, select "Digital IDs" from the left-hand menu.
- Click the "Add ID" button to start the process of creating a new digital ID.
- Choose the option to create a new digital ID.
- Select whether the digital ID will be used for digital signatures or for data encryption. For creating a digital signature, choose "Digital Signatures."
- Enter your name and email address. Optionally, you can provide other information.
- Select the key algorithm and key length for your digital ID. RSA is a common algorithm, and the key length should be at least 2048 bits for security.
- Set the options for your certificate, including the expiration date and any additional options provided.
- Enter a password to secure your digital ID. This password will be required when using the digital signature.
- Choose a location on your computer to save the digital ID file (.pfx or .p12 format).
- Complete the digital ID creation process. You may be prompted to enter the password again.
- Open the PDF document that you want to sign in Adobe Acrobat.
- Click on the "Tools" pane on the right side of the screen.
- Under the "Tools" pane, select "Sign & Certify."
- Choose "Place Signature" from the dropdown menu.
- In the "Place Signature" dialog box, select your digital ID from the list.
- Position the signature field on the document where you want your signature to appear. You can also resize the field as needed.
- Click on the signature field to sign the document. Adobe Acrobat will prompt you to enter your digital ID password to complete the signing process.
- After signing, save the document to apply the digital signature.

Verifying the digital signature

- Open the signed PDF document in Adobe Acrobat.
- Right-click on the signature field and select "Properties" to view details about the signature, including the signer's identity and timestamp.
- In the "Signature" panel, you can check the signature status. A valid signature indicates that the document has not been altered since it was signed.

Verifying the certification:

- Open the certified PDF document in Adobe Acrobat.
- Right-click on the certification signature field and select "Properties" to view details about the certification, including the signer's identity and timestamp.
- In the "Signature" panel, you can check the certification status. A valid certification indicates that the document is authentic and has not been altered since it was certified.

Chapter 8

Organizing pages and documents

Renaming, moving, and copying pages

Renaming Pages:

- Launch Adobe Acrobat and open the PDF document that contains the pages you want to rename.
- Click on "View" > "Show/Hide" > "Navigation Panes" > "Page Thumbnails" to open the Page Thumbnails panel.
- Right-click on the page you want to rename within the Page Thumbnails panel.
- Select "Page Properties" from the context menu.
- In the Page Properties dialog box, enter the new name for the page in the "Title" field.
- Click "OK" to apply the new name to the page.

Moving Pages:

- Open the PDF document in Adobe Acrobat.
- Open the Page Thumbnails panel by clicking on "View" > "Show/Hide" > "Navigation Panes" > "Page Thumbnails."
- Click on the page thumbnail(s) you want to move while holding down the Shift or Ctrl key (Windows) or Command key (Mac) to select multiple pages.
- Drag the selected pages to the desired location within the Page Thumbnails panel.
- Release the mouse button to drop the pages in the new location.

Copying Pages:

- Open the PDF document in Adobe Acrobat.
- Open the Page Thumbnails panel by clicking on "View" > "Show/Hide" > "Navigation Panes" > "Page Thumbnails."
- Click on the page thumbnail(s) you want to copy while holding down the Shift or Ctrl key (Windows) or Command key (Mac) to select multiple pages.
- Right-click on the selected pages, and choose "Copy Pages" from the context menu.
- Go to the Page Thumbnails panel and navigate to the location where you want to insert the copied pages.
- Right-click on the destination page and choose "Paste Pages" from the context menu.
- If necessary, drag the copied pages to the desired position within the Page Thumbnails panel.
- Save the document to apply the changes.

Using the Page Thumbnails pane

Opening the page thumbnails pane:

- Launch Adobe Acrobat and open the PDF document you want to work with.

- Click on "View" in the top menu.
- Choose "Show/Hide" and then select "Navigation Panes."
- Click on "Page Thumbnails" to open the Page Thumbnails pane.

Navigating and managing pages:

In the Page Thumbnails pane, you'll see thumbnails of each page in the document. Scroll through the thumbnails to view different pages.

- To change the order of pages, drag and drop a page thumbnail to a new position.
- Hold down the Shift or Ctrl key (Windows) or Command key (Mac) to select multiple pages.
- Right-click on a selected page or pages and choose "Delete" to remove them from the document.
- Right-click on a page thumbnail, choose "Insert Pages," and select the source of the pages you want to insert.
- Right-click on a page thumbnail and choose "Rotate Pages" to rotate pages clockwise or counterclockwise.
- Right-click on a selected page or pages and choose "Extract Pages" to create a new PDF with the selected pages.
- Right-click on a page thumbnail, choose "Page Properties," and set page labels for better organization.
- Double-click on a page thumbnail to navigate directly to that page.

Creating and using folders
File Explorer (Windows) or Finder (Mac):

- Open the file management application on your computer (File Explorer on Windows or Finder on Mac).
- Go to the location where your PDF files are stored.
- Right-click on an empty space within the directory and choose "New" > "Folder" (Windows) or click on "File" > "New Folder" (Mac).
- Give the folder a descriptive name.
- Drag and drop PDF files into the newly created folder or right-click on the PDF, choose "Cut" (Windows) or "Move to Trash" (Mac), navigate to the folder, and right-click to choose "Paste" (Windows) or "Move" (Mac).
- If needed, create subfolders within the main folder to further categorize your PDFs.
- You can also rename your PDF files within the folder to make them more descriptive.

Tips for Organization:

- Use clear and descriptive names for your folders to easily identify their contents.
- Adopt a consistent naming convention for your PDF files to maintain order.

- Create subfolders within folders to categorize PDFs based on topics, projects, or other criteria.
- Periodically review and organize your folders to ensure that the structure remains effective.

Organizing PDFs in the Document Cloud

- Open your web browser and go to the Adobe Document Cloud website (https://documentcloud.adobe.com/).
- Sign in to your Adobe account associated with Adobe Document Cloud. If you don't have an account, you may need to create one.
- Once signed in, you'll see a list of your documents on the Document Cloud home page.
- Upload PDFs to Adobe Document Cloud by clicking the "Upload" button. You can drag and drop files or select them from your computer.
- Organize your PDFs into folders for better categorization.
- Click on the "Create" button.
- Choose "Folder."
- Give the folder a name.
- Click "Create" to confirm.
- After creating folders, drag and drop PDFs into the appropriate folders for organization.
- Click on a file or folder to select it.
- Click again to enter edit mode and rename it.
- Share individual PDFs or entire folders with others for collaborative work.
- Open Adobe Acrobat on your computer.
- Go to "File" > "Open" > "Document Cloud."
- Access your organized PDFs directly from Adobe Acrobat.
- Collaborate on PDFs in real-time using the commenting and reviewing features in Adobe Acrobat.
- Access your PDFs and folders from various devices, as Adobe Document Cloud syncs your content across platforms.
- Leverage Adobe Document Cloud's security features, such as password protection and encryption, to ensure the confidentiality of your documents.
- Adobe Document Cloud retains version history, allowing you to revert to previous document versions if needed.
- Install the Adobe Acrobat Reader mobile app on your iOS or Android device to access and organize your PDFs on the go.

Managing files in the Home view
Accessing Home View:

- Open your web browser and go to the Adobe Document Cloud website (https://documentcloud.adobe.com/).

- Sign in to your Adobe account associated with Adobe Document Cloud. If you don't have an account, you may need to create one.

Managing files:

- Click on the "Upload" button to upload PDF files from your computer.
- You can drag and drop files or use the file selection dialog to choose the files you want to upload.
- Click on the "Create" button.
- Choose "Folder" to create a new folder.
- Name the folder and click "Create" to confirm.
- Drag and drop files into folders to organize them.
- Click on a file, drag it over the desired folder, and release the mouse button to move the file.
- Click on a file or folder to select it.
- Click again to enter edit mode and rename it.
- Select the file or folder you want to delete.
- Click on the "More options" (three dots) icon and choose "Delete."

Searching and indexing documents

Searching documents:

Basic search:

- Open the PDF document you want to search in Adobe Acrobat.
- Locate the search bar typically found in the upper-right corner.
- Enter the keyword or phrase you want to search for.
- Acrobat will highlight instances of the search term within the document.
- Navigate through the results using the arrows in the search bar.

Advanced search

- Click on the small triangle next to the search bar to open the advanced search panel.
- Enter specific search criteria, such as words, phrases, or document properties.
- Refine your search using options like whole words, case-sensitive, or stemming.
- The advanced search panel will display a list of search results.
- Click on a result to jump directly to that location in the document.

Indexing documents:

- Go to "Edit" > "Preferences" (Windows) or "Acrobat" > "Preferences" (Mac).
- In the Preferences dialog box, select "Search" in the left pane.
- Check the box that says "Enable searching the currently open PDF document for faster results."
- Click "OK" to apply the changes and close the Preferences dialog.

Indexing status:

- After enabling indexing, you may see an indexing status message at the bottom of the document window.
- Allow some time for Acrobat to index the document.

Search with indexing:

- Enter your search term in the search bar as usual.
- With indexing enabled, Acrobat will leverage the index for faster and more efficient searches.

Manage indexing preferences:

- If needed, you can go back to the Preferences dialog and adjust indexing preferences.
- Access Preferences through "Edit" > "Preferences" (Windows) or "Acrobat" > "Preferences" (Mac).

Tips for efficient searching:

- Use specific and relevant keywords to get accurate search results.
- Experiment with advanced search options to refine and narrow down results.
- For scanned documents, run OCR (Optical Character Recognition) to make the text searchable.
- When applicable, enable the "Whole words only" option to avoid partial matches.
- Use the case-sensitive option if you need to distinguish between uppercase and lowercase letters.
- If you frequently update documents, consider regularly updating and rebuilding the index for optimal search performance.

Using search tools and filters

Adobe Acrobat provides powerful search tools and filters to help you efficiently locate information within PDF documents. Follwop the guide below:

Basic search:

- Launch Adobe Acrobat and open the PDF document you want to search.
- Locate the search bar, usually at the top-right corner of the interface.
- Type your search terms into the search bar.
- Acrobat will highlight instances of the search term within the document.
- Use the arrows in the search bar to navigate through the results.

Advanced search:

- Click on the small triangle next to the search bar to open the advanced search panel.
- Enter specific search criteria, such as words, phrases, or document properties.

- Refine your search using options like whole words, case-sensitive, or stemming (finding variations of a word).
- The advanced search panel will display a list of search results.
- Click on a result to jump directly to that location in the document.

Search Filters:

- In the Comments pane, you can filter search results by annotations like comments, highlights, or sticky notes.
- Use filters to narrow down results based on document properties such as title, author, subject, etc.
- If your PDF contains scanned images, run OCR to make the text searchable.
- Go to "Tools" > "Enhance Scans" > "Recognize Text."

Tips for efficient searching

- Use specific and relevant keywords to get accurate search results.
- Experiment with advanced search options to refine and narrow down results.
- Use the case-sensitive option if you need to distinguish between uppercase and lowercase letters.

Search across multiple PDFs:

- If you have multiple PDFs in a portfolio, you can use the search feature across all documents in the portfolio.
- Combine multiple PDFs into a single document for a unified search experience.

Redaction search:

- Use the redaction tool to search for and redact specific content within a document.

Cloud search:

- If your PDFs are stored in Adobe Document Cloud, use the web interface for cloud-based search features.

Creating an index for large document collections

- Ensure all the documents you want to include in the index are accessible and organized in a single folder.
- Open Adobe Acrobat and create a new PDF document that will serve as your index.
- Open each document you want to include in the index.
- Identify key sections or topics in each document.
- Use the "Bookmarks" panel to add bookmarks to these sections.

- Open the "View" menu, choose "Show/Hide," and select "Navigation Panes" > "Bookmarks" to access the Bookmarks panel.
- Click on the desired location in the document, right-click, and choose "New Bookmark."

Name bookmarks

- Rename the bookmarks to correspond to the sections or topics they represent.
- Right-click on a bookmark, choose "Properties," and enter a descriptive name.
- Within your index document, create hyperlinks that point to the corresponding bookmarks in each document.
- Go to the "Edit" menu, select "Link," and choose "Add or Edit Web or Document Link."
- Draw a rectangle around the text you want to hyperlink and choose the "Go to a page view" option, selecting the appropriate bookmark.

Add page numbers:

- Include page numbers in your index document to indicate where each section starts.
- Use the "Text Box" tool to add page numbers next to each hyperlink.
- Test the hyperlinks in your index document to ensure they navigate to the correct sections in the other documents.
- Save your index document with a descriptive name.
- If needed, share or distribute the index document along with the individual documents to provide an organized navigation structure.

Printing and exporting

Printing a PDF document:

- Launch Adobe Acrobat and open the PDF document you want to print.
- Go to the "File" menu and select "Print" or use the keyboard shortcut (Ctrl+P on Windows, Command+P on Mac).
- In the Print dialog, select the printer you want to use.
- Configure print settings such as page range, number of copies, and page size.
- Use the "Preview" option to see how the document will look when printed.
- Adjust settings if needed.
- Click the "Print" button to start the printing process.

Export as another file format:

- Open the PDF document in Adobe Acrobat.
- Go to the "File" menu, select "Export," and choose the desired file format (e.g., Microsoft Word, Excel, PowerPoint).
- Select the file format you want to export the PDF as.

- Configure export settings, such as choosing specific pages or adjusting layout options.
- Enter a file name and choose the destination where the exported file will be saved.
- Click the "Save" or "Export" button to complete the export process.

Save as Image:

- Open the PDF document in Adobe Acrobat.
- Go to the "File" menu, select "Export," and choose "Image."
- Choose the image format (e.g., JPEG, PNG) and adjust image settings.
- Enter a file name and choose the destination where the image files will be saved.
- Click the "Save" or "Export" button to save the PDF pages as images.
- Use the print preview feature to ensure the document will print as expected.
- When printing or exporting, you can specify a custom page range to include only specific pages.
- When exporting as an image, consider adjusting compression settings to balance file size and image quality.
- Some PDFs may have security settings that restrict printing or exporting. Ensure you have the necessary permissions.
- Be aware of any watermarks or headers/footers that may be included during printing or exporting.
- Adobe Acrobat also provides batch processing tools that allow you to apply printing or exporting actions to multiple PDFs simultaneously.

Chapter 8

Printing options and settings

Print dialog options and print presets

Follow the steps below:

- Open Adobe Acrobat and open the PDF file you want to print.
- Click on the "File" menu in the top-left corner.
- In the drop-down menu, choose the "Print" option. You can also use the keyboard shortcut (Ctrl+P on Windows or Command+P on Mac).
- The Print dialog box will open. Here, you can find various print settings.
- Look for options like "Page Range," "Copies," and "Page Sizing & Handling." Adjust these settings based on your printing needs.
- There may be a button or link like "Advanced" or "More Options" that allows you to access additional print settings.
- Some versions of Adobe Acrobat provide the option to save and use print presets. Look for a dropdown menu or a separate section that allows you to choose or manage presets.
- If you want to save a specific set of print settings as a preset, look for an option like "Save As" or "Save Preset." This allows you to reuse these settings for future prints.

Troubleshooting common printing issues

Follow the steps below:

- **Check printer connection:** Ensure that your printer is properly connected to your computer and turned on. If it's a wireless printer, make sure it's connected to the same network.
- **Update printer drivers:** Make sure you have the latest drivers for your printer installed on your computer. Visit the printer manufacturer's website to download and install the latest drivers.
- **Check printer queue:** Open the printer queue to check if there are any stuck or pending print jobs. Cancel any jobs that may be causing issues and try printing again.
- **Restart printer and computer:** Sometimes, simply restarting your printer and computer can resolve printing issues. Turn off both devices, wait a few seconds, and then turn them back on.
- **Update Adobe Acrobat:** Ensure that you are using the latest version of Adobe Acrobat. Updates may include bug fixes and improvements that can address printing issues.
- **Print a different document:** Try printing a different PDF document or a different type of file to see if the issue is specific to one document or file type.
- **Print as image:** In the print dialog box, you may find an option to "Print as Image." This can sometimes resolve printing problems related to fonts or graphics. It's usually located in the "Advanced" settings.

- **Check page size and orientation:** Ensure that the page size and orientation selected in the print settings match the size and orientation of the paper loaded in the printer.
- **Clear the print cache:** Clear the print spooler cache. Go to the "Devices and Printers" settings, right-click on your printer, and select "See what's printing." From the menu, choose "Cancel All Documents." Then, restart the computer and try printing again.
- **Adjust print settings:** In the Adobe Acrobat print dialog, review and adjust settings such as page scaling, color management, and resolution as needed.
- **Reinstall Adobe Acrobat:** If the issue persists, try uninstalling and reinstalling Adobe Acrobat. This can help resolve any software-related problems.
- **Check for PDF corruption:** If the issue is specific to one PDF file, try opening and printing a different PDF. If other PDFs print successfully, the original file may be corrupted.

Exporting PDFs to different formats
Follow the steps below:

Export PDF to Microsoft Word:

- Open the PDF file in Adobe Acrobat.
- Click on the "File" menu.
- Select "Export."
- Choose "Microsoft Word" as the export format.
- Select the desired settings and click "Export."

Export PDF to Microsoft Excel:

- Open the PDF file in Adobe Acrobat.
- Click on the "File" menu.
- Select "Export."
- Choose "Microsoft Excel" as the export format.
- Adjust settings if needed and click "Export."

Export PDF to PowerPoint:

- Open the PDF file in Adobe Acrobat.
- Click on the "File" menu.
- Select "Export."
- Choose "Microsoft PowerPoint" as the export format.
- Adjust settings if needed and click "Export."

Export PDF to Image Formats (JPEG, PNG, etc.)

- Open the PDF file in Adobe Acrobat.
- Click on the "File" menu.
- Select "Export."
- Choose "Image" as the export format.
- Select the image format you want (JPEG, PNG, etc.).
- Adjust settings if needed and click "Export."

Export PDF to Text:

- Open the PDF file in Adobe Acrobat.
- Click on the "File" menu.
- Select "Export."
- Choose "Text" as the export format.
- Adjust settings if needed and click "Export."

Export PDF to HTML:

- Open the PDF file in Adobe Acrobat.
- Click on the "File" menu.
- Select "Export."
- Choose "HTML" as the export format.
- Adjust settings if needed and click "Export."

Export PDF to Rich Text Format (RTF):

- Open the PDF file in Adobe Acrobat.
- Click on the "File" menu.
- Select "Export."
- Choose "Rich Text Format" as the export format.
- Adjust settings if needed and click "Export."

Export PDF to Other Formats:

- Open the PDF file in Adobe Acrobat.
- Click on the "File" menu.
- Select "Export."
- Choose "More Formats" to see additional options.
- Select the desired export format and adjust settings if needed.
- Click "Export."

Optimizing PDFs for web and mobile viewing
Follow the steps below:

Optimizing for web:

- Launch Adobe Acrobat and open the PDF file you want to optimize.
- Navigate to the "File" menu and select "Save As Other." Choose "Optimized PDF..."
- In the "Make compatible with" dropdown, choose the latest version of Acrobat that your audience is likely to have. This ensures compatibility with various PDF viewers.
- Click on the "Settings" button next to "Adobe PDF Preset." Choose "Smallest File Size" or adjust the settings manually based on your needs.
- In the "Images" tab, adjust the compression settings for color, grayscale, and monochrome images. Lowering the resolution and quality can significantly reduce file size.
- In the "Fonts" tab, choose "Embed all fonts" to ensure font consistency across different devices.
- In the "Discard Objects" tab, select options like "Discard All Alternate Images" and "Discard User Data" if applicable.
- Click on the "Advanced" tab to access additional optimization options. For web viewing, you might want to consider options like optimizing for fast web view.
- After adjusting the settings, click "OK" to apply the changes. Save the optimized PDF with a new name to keep the original file intact.

When optimizing for mobile, the goal is to ensure a responsive and fast-loading experience. Follow similar steps as above, but consider the following additional points:

- Ensure that the PDF layout is responsive to different screen sizes. Use a single-column layout and avoid fixed-width elements.
- Optimize font sizes for readability on smaller screens. Test the document on different devices to ensure text is legible.
- Check interactive elements like links and buttons to ensure they work well on touch screens.
- Follow the steps mentioned for web optimization to reduce the file size, which is crucial for mobile devices with limited bandwidth.
- Test the optimized PDF on various mobile devices to ensure a seamless viewing experience.

Advanced Editing and Formatting

Advanced Editing:

- Click on the "Edit PDF" tool in the toolbar to select and edit text and images directly within the PDF.
- Use the "Link" tool to add or edit hyperlinks within the document. This is useful for creating clickable links to websites, pages within the document, or email addresses.
- Go to "Tools" > "Edit PDF" > "Header & Footer" to insert headers and footers into the PDF for consistent page numbering or other information.
- Use the "Watermark" tool to add text or image watermarks to your PDF for branding or security purposes.

- The "Redaction" tool allows you to permanently remove sensitive information from the document. This is crucial for protecting confidential data.
- Bates numbering is useful for legal professionals. You can add Bates numbering to PDF documents using the "Header & Footer" tool.
- Use the "Prepare Form" tool to create interactive forms. You can add text fields, checkboxes, radio buttons, and more.
- In the "Edit PDF" tool, you can select and manipulate individual objects, such as text boxes and images. Right-click to access advanced object editing options.

Advanced Formatting:

- The "Format" panel (accessible through the "Edit PDF" tool) allows you to adjust font type, size, color, and other formatting options.
- Use the "Edit PDF" tool to adjust paragraph formatting, including alignment, line spacing, and indentation.
- Acrobat provides tools to edit tables within a PDF. You can add or remove rows and columns, and adjust cell properties.
- Select the "Edit PDF" tool, right-click on an image, and choose "Edit Image" to access advanced image editing options.
- In the "Edit PDF" tool, you can adjust color settings for text, objects, and backgrounds.

Chapter 9

Advanced text and image editing tools

Using the Content Editing panel for precise edits

Content editing panel:

- Launch Adobe Acrobat and open the PDF file you want to edit.
- Locate and open the "Content Editing" panel. This panel may be accessed through the "Tools" pane on the right side of the screen. Look for options such as "Edit PDF" or "Content Editing."
- Within the Content Editing panel, select the "Edit Text & Images" tool. This tool allows you to make precise edits to text and images in the PDF.
- Use the tool to select the text or image you want to edit. Click on the text or image to highlight it.
- Once the text or image is selected, you can make various edits. For text, you can edit the content, change font properties, adjust size, and more. For images, you can move, resize, or replace the image.
- If you are editing text, you can access the text attributes by right-clicking on the selected text and choosing "Properties." This allows you to modify font, size, color, and other text attributes.
- Explore the options available in the Content Editing panel for more advanced editing. This may include aligning objects, distributing objects, grouping items, and more.
- The Content Editing panel may offer options to rotate or flip selected objects. This can be useful for adjusting the orientation of text or images.
- After making the desired edits, save your changes. You can save the edited document with a new name to keep the original file intact.

Working with advanced image editing features

Image Editing in Adobe Acrobat:

- Launch Adobe Acrobat and open the PDF file containing the image you want to edit.
- In the toolbar on the right, click on the "Edit PDF" tool. This tool allows you to make changes to the content within the PDF, including images.
- Click on the image you want to edit. This should highlight the image and provide handles for resizing.
- Right-click on the selected image, and you may see options such as "Edit Image" or "Image Editing." Selecting these options allows you to perform various image-related tasks.
- If available, you can use the cropping tool to crop the image to a specific area. You can also resize the image by dragging the handles.
- Some versions of Adobe Acrobat allow you to rotate or flip the selected image. Look for these options in the context menu or toolbar.
- If you want to replace the existing image with a new one, you may find an option to "Replace Image" or "Swap Image" in the image editing menu.

- Explore options to adjust image properties such as brightness, contrast, and color if available.
- For accessibility purposes, you may want to add alternative text to describe the image. Right-click on the image and look for options related to alt text or image properties.
- Depending on the version of Adobe Acrobat, there may be additional features for image editing. Explore the menus and context options for any advanced image-related functions.
- After making the desired image edits, save your changes. Remember that saving the PDF with edits will overwrite the original file.

Limitations:

- Adobe Acrobat is not a dedicated image editing tool, so its capabilities are limited compared to software like Adobe Photoshop.
- Some advanced features may only be available for specific image formats. Check the compatibility of your image format with the features you want to use.
- For more advanced image editing, consider using Adobe Photoshop or another dedicated image editing tool.

Working with layers

- In Adobe Acrobat, you can view the Layers pane by going to the "View" menu and selecting "Show/Hide" > "Navigation Panes" > "Layers."
- If your PDF document contains layers, you'll see them listed in the Layers pane. Layers might include annotations, comments, stamps, or other elements that can be toggled on or off.
- Toggle the visibility of layers by clicking on the eye icon next to each layer. This allows you to control which layers are visible or hidden.
- You can rearrange the order of layers by dragging them up or down in the Layers pane. This affects the stacking order of elements on the page.
- When adding comments or annotations (such as text boxes, shapes, or highlights), Acrobat may create layers for these elements automatically. You can control the visibility of these layers.
- Right-click on a layer in the Layers pane to access additional options. Depending on your version of Acrobat, you might have options to change layer properties, including color, opacity, and other settings.
- If you want to merge or flatten layers, go to the "Tools" menu, choose "Print Production," and select "Flattener Preview." From here, you can choose options for flattening layers when printing.

Creating and managing layers in PDFs
Viewing Layers in Adobe Acrobat:

- Go to the "View" menu and select "Show/Hide" > "Navigation Panes" > "Layers" to open the Layers pane.
- If your PDF document contains layers, they will be listed in the Layers pane. Layers may include annotations, stamps, or other elements.

Managing Comments and Annotations:

- Use the "Comment" tools to add annotations, highlights, text comments, etc. Each type of comment may be considered a separate layer.
- In the Layers pane, you can toggle the visibility of comment layers on or off by clicking the eye icon next to each layer.
- You can move comments up or down in the stacking order by dragging them in the Layers pane.
- Right-click on a comment layer in the Layers pane to access options for changing its properties, such as color, opacity, etc.

Stamps and Watermarks:

- Use the "Stamp" tool or "Watermark" tool to add stamps or watermarks to your PDF. Each stamp or watermark may be on a separate layer.
- Toggle the visibility of stamp layers in the Layers pane.
- Right-click on a stamp layer to access options for adjusting properties like color, opacity, etc.
- If you need to merge or flatten layers for printing or other purposes, you can use the "Print Production" tools. Go to the "Tools" menu, select "Print Production," and choose "Flattener Preview."
- In the Flattener Preview, you can choose options for flattening layers. This process merges visible layers into a single layer.

Layer visibility and export options
Layer visibility:

- Go to the "View" menu, choose "Show/Hide," and then select "Navigation Panes" > "Layers" to open the Layers pane.
- If your PDF document contains layers, they will be listed in the Layers pane. Layers might include annotations, stamps, or other elements.
- Click the eye icon next to each layer in the Layers pane to toggle the visibility on or off. This allows you to control which layers are visible or hidden.

Export Options:

- If you want to export a specific layer or a visible combination of layers, you can use the "Export" feature. Go to the "File" menu, select "Export," and then choose "Image." In the export settings, you can select the pages and choose to export all visible layers.
- If you need to flatten layers for printing or other purposes, you can use the "Print Production" tools. Go to the "Tools" menu, select "Print Production," and choose "Flattener Preview." In the Flattener Preview, you can choose options for flattening layers.
- Adobe Acrobat's layer functionality is often related to comments, annotations, stamps, and watermarks rather than traditional graphic design layers.
- If you are looking for more advanced layer management and export options, especially for graphic design purposes, you might need to use dedicated graphic design software such as Adobe Illustrator or Photoshop.

Using the content editing panel

Open the Content Editing Panel:

- Launch Adobe Acrobat and open the PDF document you want to edit.
- In the right-hand Tools pane, click on "Edit PDF" to expand the tools. Within the Edit PDF tools, you may find the "Content Editing" panel.

Edit text:

- In the Content Editing panel, select the "Edit Text & Images" tool.
- Click on the text you want to edit. A bounding box will appear around the text.
- You can now add, delete, or modify the text.
- Use the formatting options in the toolbar to adjust font size, color, and other attributes.

Edit images:

- In the Content Editing panel, select the "Edit Text & Images" tool.
- Click on the image you want to edit. A bounding box will appear around the image.
- You can now move, resize, or replace the image. Right-click on the image for additional options.

Edit Fonts and Formatting:

- Use the formatting options in the toolbar to adjust font attributes such as size, color, and style.
- Adjust paragraph attributes, such as alignment and line spacing.

In the Content Editing panel, you may find the "Edit Object" tool. This tool allows you to select and manipulate individual objects, such as text boxes and images. Right-click for advanced editing options. Once you've made the desired edits, save the document. Click on "File" and choose "Save" or "Save As."

Advanced formatting options and settings

Page layout and margins:

- Go to "File" > "Properties" > "Description" tab. You can change the page size under the "Page Size" section.
- Navigate to "File" > "Properties" > "Layout" tab. Here, you can adjust margins and orientation.

Text formatting:

- When saving a PDF, you can embed fonts to ensure consistent display across devices. Go to "File" > "Save As Other" > "More Options" > "Adobe PDF Settings." Under the "Fonts" tab, choose "Embed all fonts."
- Use the "Edit PDF" tool to select text, right-click, and choose "Properties" to adjust font size, color, and other attributes.

Annotations and comments:

- In the "Comment" pane, right-click on a comment and choose "Properties" to customize the appearance of comments, including author name, color, and icon style.
- If there are many comments, go to "Comments" > "Summarize Comments" to create a summary document with comments listed.

Advanced editing options:

- Use the "Edit Object" tool in the "Content Editing" panel to select and manipulate individual objects, such as images and text boxes.
- In the "Edit PDF" tool, right-click on an image and choose "Edit Image" to access advanced image editing options.

Accessibility:

- Right-click on an image, choose "Edit Alternate Text," and add descriptive alt text for accessibility.
- Go to "Tools" > "Accessibility" > "Full Check" to review and fix accessibility issues.

Form fields:

- In the "Prepare Form" tool, select a form field, right-click, and choose "Properties" to customize field properties, such as appearance and actions.
- Use the "Distribute" and "Align" tools in the "Prepare Form" panel to organize and align form fields.

Security:

- Go to "File" > "Properties" > "Security" tab to set password protection and encryption options.

Advanced printing options:

- In the Print dialog box, choose "Advanced" and enable "Print as Image" to resolve printing issues related to fonts or graphics.

Document properties

- Go to "File" > "Properties" to view and edit document metadata, including title, author, subject, and keywords.

Leveraging the Content Editing tools for complex edits

- Launch Adobe Acrobat and open the PDF document you want to edit.
- In the right-hand Tools pane, click on "Edit PDF" to expand the tools. Within the Edit PDF tools, you will find the "Content Editing" panel.
- In the Content Editing panel, choose the "Edit Text & Images" tool.
- Click on the text you want to edit. A bounding box will appear around the text.
- You can now add, delete, or modify the text.
- Use the formatting options in the toolbar to adjust font size, color, and other attributes.
- In the Content Editing panel, select the "Edit Text & Images" tool.
- Click on the image you want to edit. A bounding box will appear around the image.
- You can now move, resize, or replace the image. Right-click on the image for additional options.
- In the Content Editing panel, select the "TouchUp Text" tool.
- Click on individual characters to edit or move them.
- In the Content Editing panel, select the "Edit Object" tool.
- Click on images or objects to select and edit them individually.
- Right-click for additional options such as "Edit Image" for more advanced image editing.
- In the Content Editing panel, choose the "Link" tool.
- Click and drag to create a link or modify existing links.
- In the Content Editing panel, choose the "Prepare Form" tool.
- Click on the "Add New Field" button to add form fields or select existing fields to edit.
- Use the "Edit Object" tool to adjust the stacking order of text and images. Right-click on an object and choose "Bring to Front" or "Send to Back."
- Once you've made the desired edits, save the document. Click on "File" and choose "Save" or "Save As."

Chapter 10

Introduction to JavaScript in Acrobat

Basics of JavaScript for Acrobat

JavaScript Console:

- Open the JavaScript Console:
- In Adobe Acrobat, go to "View" > "Show/Hide" > "Toolbar Items" > "JavaScript Console."

Document-level JavaScript:

- Click on the "Console" tab in the JavaScript Console window. This is where you can add document-level JavaScript that applies to the entire document.

Field-level JavaScript:

- In form editing mode, right-click on a form field and choose "Properties."

Events and actions:

- Events like "Mouse Up," "Mouse Down," "Blur," etc., can trigger actions.

JavaScript in Acrobat Forms:

- Go to "Tools" > "Prepare Form."

Accessing the JavaScript Console

- Launch Adobe Acrobat on your computer.
- Go to the "View" menu.
- Choose "Show/Hide" from the "View" menu.
- In the "Toolbar Items" submenu, select "JavaScript Console" to enable the JavaScript Console.
- Once enabled, you should see the JavaScript Console as a separate pane or toolbar within Adobe Acrobat.
- In the JavaScript Console, you can enter JavaScript code directly.
- Press "Enter" to run the code, and the console will display the output or any error messages.

Creating custom actions and scripts

Follow the steps below:

- Launch Adobe Acrobat on your computer.
- Go to the "Tools" pane on the right side of the screen.
- Click on "Action Wizard" to open the Action Wizard panel.
- In the Action Wizard panel, click on "New Action."

- Choose the steps you want to include in your custom action. Steps can include tasks like adding a watermark, running JavaScript, or extracting pages.
- Configure each step according to your requirements. For example, if you're adding a watermark, specify the watermark text, font, and position.
- Once you've configured the steps, click "Save" to save the custom action.
- Select the custom action in the Action Wizard panel and click "Start" to run the action on your PDF.

Creating and running custom JavaScript actions

- Launch Adobe Acrobat on your computer.
- Go to the "View" menu and select "Show/Hide" > "Toolbar Items" > "JavaScript Console."
- In the JavaScript Console, click on the icon that looks like a notepad to create a new JavaScript action.
- Enter your JavaScript code in the editor. For example, you can use the following simple script to add a text annotation to the current page:
- Click on the save icon in the JavaScript Console to save your custom JavaScript action. Save it with a meaningful name.
- If the JavaScript Console is not already open, go to the "View" menu and select "Show/Hide" > "Toolbar Items" > "JavaScript Console."
- Click on the folder icon in the JavaScript Console to load a JavaScript action.
- Choose the JavaScript action you previously created from the list.
- Click on the play icon to run the selected JavaScript action.

Attaching JavaScript to Form Elements or Actions

- Go to "Tools" > "Prepare Form" to enter form editing mode.
- Right-click on a form element (e.g., text field, button) and choose "Properties."
- In the Properties dialog, go to the "Actions" tab.
- Choose an event (e.g., "Mouse Up," "Blur") and select "Run a JavaScript" as the action. Enter your JavaScript code.
- Click "Close" to close the Properties dialog, and save the document.

Troubleshooting JavaScript errors

- Open the JavaScript Console by going to the "View" menu, selecting "Show/Hide," and choosing "Toolbar Items" > "JavaScript Console." Look for error messages in the console. If there are syntax errors or runtime errors, they will be displayed here.
- Ensure that your JavaScript code follows proper syntax rules. Common syntax issues include missing semicolons, parentheses, or brackets. Use a text editor with syntax highlighting to make it easier to identify syntax errors.

- Check the logical flow of your script. Ensure that variables are declared before use and that functions are defined before they are called. Use comments to annotate your code and make it easier to understand.
- Temporarily comment out sections of your code to isolate the problematic area. This can help you pinpoint the source of the error. Gradually uncomment sections and test to identify when the error occurs.
- Insert console.println() statements to print variable values or intermediate results to the JavaScript Console. This can help you understand the state of variables at different points in your script.
- Insert app.alert() statements to create pop-up alerts with messages or variable values. This is a simple way to debug your script.
- Adobe Acrobat has a built-in debugger that can help you step through your code. To use it, open the JavaScript Console, go to the "Debugger" tab, and set breakpoints in your code.
- Ensure that the JavaScript features you are using are supported by the version of Adobe Acrobat you are using. Check the Adobe Acrobat JavaScript Scripting Reference for information on supported features and changes between versions.
- Refer to the official Adobe Acrobat documentation and JavaScript scripting reference for guidance on best practices and troubleshooting. Visit Adobe user forums or communities to seek help from other users who may have encountered similar issues.

Optimizing PDFs for Accessibility

- Open your PDF in Adobe Acrobat.
- Go to "View" > "Tools" > "Accessibility."
- In the Accessibility Tools pane, select "Full Check."
- Follow the prompts to run a full accessibility check.
- Review and address any issues identified in the accessibility report.

Add document structure:

- In the Accessibility Tools pane, select "Add Tags to Document."
- Acrobat will attempt to tag the document automatically. Review and correct any tagging issues.
- Select the "Reading Order" tool in the Accessibility Tools pane.
- Right-click on an image and choose "Edit Alternate Text." Provide descriptive alternative text for each image.
- Apply proper heading styles to headings in your document.
- Use styles for formatting text instead of manual formatting.
- Select the "Edit" tool in the Accessibility Tools pane.
- Right-click on a link and choose "Create Link."
- Provide meaningful link text.
- Use the "Reading Order" tool to adjust the reading order of elements.
- Ensure that the reading order matches the logical order of the content.

- Use the "Lists" tool to create ordered or unordered lists. Use the "Table Editor" tool to tag tables and ensure proper reading order.
- Go to "File" > "Properties." In the Document Properties dialog, go to the "Advanced" tab. Set the document language under "Reading Options."
- Use the "TouchUp Reading Order" tool to select text. Right-click and choose "Properties." Check the color contrast.
- Go to "File" > "Properties." In the Document Properties dialog, go to the "Description" tab. Set the language in the "Language" field.
- Use the "Bookmarks" tool to add bookmarks for navigation. Make sure bookmarks have meaningful names.
- Go to "Tools" > "Forms." Use the "Run Form Field Recognition" tool to ensure form fields are accessible.
- In the Accessibility Tools pane, select "Accessibility Checker." Choose "Options" and select the "ISO 14289-1 (PDF/UA)" standard. Run the accessibility check using the PDF/UA standard.
- Go to "View" > "Tools" > "Accessibility." In the Accessibility Tools pane, select "Touch Up Reading Order." Right-click and choose "Accessibility" > "Quick Check" to validate accessibility.
- Test your document with screen reader software to ensure compatibility and usability. Adobe Acrobat provides a "Read Out Loud" feature for basic testing.
- Check for Updates: Ensure you are using the latest version of Adobe Acrobat for the most up-to-date accessibility features. Regularly test your documents with accessibility tools to identify and address issues. Consult Documentation: Refer to Adobe Acrobat documentation for detailed information on accessibility features.

Chapter 11

Making PDFs accessible to users with disabilities

Overview of accessibility standards and guidelines

- **PDF/UA (ISO 14289-1):** PDF/UA, which stands for "Universal Accessibility," is an ISO standard specifically designed for ensuring the accessibility of PDF documents. It provides guidelines for creating accessible PDF files, including proper tagging, navigation, and other elements to make documents accessible to users with disabilities.

- **WCAG (Web Content Accessibility Guidelines):** While not specific to Adobe Acrobat, WCAG is a widely recognized set of guidelines for web content accessibility. Many of the principles and techniques outlined in WCAG can be applied to PDF documents. The latest version is WCAG 2.1, and it includes criteria for making web content, including PDFs, accessible.

- **Section 508:** In the United States, Section 508 of the Rehabilitation Act outlines accessibility requirements for electronic and information technology, including PDF documents. The standards for Section 508 were updated to align with WCAG 2.0, making accessibility more consistent across different technologies.

- **Adobe PDF Accessibility Checker (PAC):** Adobe Acrobat includes a built-in Accessibility Checker tool that helps users identify and fix accessibility issues in PDF documents. This tool checks against the PDF/UA standard and provides feedback on areas that need improvement.

- **Tagged PDFs:** Properly tagging PDF documents is essential for accessibility. Tags define the structure of the document, making it easier for screen readers to interpret and present information to users. Tags should accurately represent the document's structure, such as headings, paragraphs, lists, tables, and more.

- **Alternative text for images:** Images in PDFs should include alternative text to provide a meaningful description for users who cannot see the visual content. This is crucial for conveying information conveyed through images.

- **Logical Reading order:** The reading order of content should be logical and consistent with the document's visual layout. This ensures that screen readers can present information in a way that makes sense to users.

- **Interactive elements accessibility:** Forms, links, and other interactive elements within PDFs should be designed and tagged to be accessible. This includes providing descriptive text for form fields and ensuring that interactive elements are keyboard accessible.

- **Bookmarks and navigation:** PDFs should include bookmarks and navigational aids to help users easily move through the document. Bookmarks can provide a structured overview of the content, aiding in efficient navigation.

Understanding the needs of users with disabilities

The considerations below will prove helpful in this regard:

- **Screen reader compatibility:** Many users with visual impairments rely on screen readers to access digital content. Ensuring that PDF documents are properly tagged and structured is crucial for screen reader compatibility. Tags help convey the document's structure, such as headings, paragraphs, lists, and more.
- **Alternative text for images:** Users with visual impairments cannot see images, so providing alternative text (alt text) for images is essential. Alt text should convey the meaning or information conveyed by the images.
- **Keyboard accessibility:** Some users with mobility impairments may navigate using keyboards instead of a mouse. Designing PDF forms and interactive elements to be fully keyboard accessible ensures that all users can interact with the content.
- **High Contrast and color choices:** Users with low vision or color blindness may have difficulty distinguishing between certain colors. Ensure there is sufficient color contrast, and avoid conveying important information solely through color. Use differentiating patterns, shapes, or labels as well.
- **Text size and font choices:** Users with visual impairments may require larger text sizes or specific font choices for better readability. Adobe Acrobat allows users to zoom in on documents, but ensuring that the default text size is reasonable is important.
- **Logical reading order:** The reading order of content should follow a logical sequence, making it easier for users with screen readers or other assistive technologies to understand the document's structure and content flow.
- **Accessible forms:** Forms within PDFs should be designed with accessibility in mind. This includes properly labeling form fields, providing instructions, and ensuring that users can navigate through the form using assistive technologies.
- **Interactive elements:** Ensure that interactive elements, such as buttons and links, are accessible to users who rely on keyboards or screen readers. Provide clear and concise instructions for these elements.
- **Document language specification:** Specify the document language to assist screen readers in pronunciation and language-specific processing.
- **Accessible tables:** If your PDF contains tables, ensure they are properly tagged, and header cells are identified. This helps screen readers interpret and present tabular information accurately.
- **Testing with users:** Conduct usability testing with individuals who have various disabilities to identify potential barriers and gather feedback on the accessibility of your PDF documents.
- **Accessibility checker:** Use the built-in Accessibility Checker in Adobe Acrobat to identify and address potential accessibility issues in your documents. The tool provides feedback on areas that need improvement.

Using tags and structure elements

Tags and structure elements in Adobe Acrobat are essential for creating accessible PDF documents. Properly tagging a PDF means associating structural information with the content, allowing assistive technologies like screen readers to interpret and present the information in a meaningful way. The tips below can guide you on how to use tags and structure elements in Adobe Acrobat:

Access the tags pane:

- Open your PDF document in Adobe Acrobat.
- Go to the "View" menu and select "Show/Hide" > "Navigation Panes" > "Tags" to open the Tags pane.

Tagging content:

- Use the "Add Tags to Document" feature to automatically add tags based on the document's structure. Go to "Tools" > "Accessibility" > "Add Tags to Document."
- Manually tag content by right-clicking on elements in the document and selecting "Properties." In the Properties dialog, go to the "Tag" tab and choose the appropriate tag type.

Tag types:

Common tag types include:

- Heading Tags (H1, H2, etc.): Use for headings to provide document structure.
- P (Paragraph): Use for regular text paragraphs.
- Table: Use for tables.
- Figure and Figure/Caption: Use for images and their captions.
- Link: Use for hyperlinks.
- List Item (LI): Use for list items within ordered or unordered lists.

Tagging tables:

- For tables, ensure that each cell is tagged appropriately. Right-click on the table tag in the Tags pane and choose "Properties" to specify header cells and other details.

Tagging images:

- Tag images using the "Figure" tag. Provide alternative text for images by right-clicking on the image tag and selecting "Properties."

Setting reading order:

The order of tags in the Tags pane determines the reading order for screen readers. Arrange tags in the correct reading order to ensure a logical flow of content.

Checking tags and structure:

Use the "Accessibility Checker" under the "Tools" menu to identify and fix tagging issues. The checker will report any problems with the document's structure and offer suggestions for improvement.

Adjusting tag structure:

If needed, you can manually adjust the tag structure by dragging and dropping tags within the Tags pane to create a logical hierarchy.

Document language specification:

Specify the document language in the document properties to assist screen readers in proper pronunciation and language-specific processing.

Tagging links:

Ensure that hyperlinks are tagged correctly. Right-click on the link, select "Properties," and choose the appropriate tag type.

Adding and editing tags for accessibility

Tags for accessibility in Adobe Acrobat is crucial for ensuring that PDF documents are accessible to users with disabilities. Tags provide structural information to assistive technologies, making it possible for screen readers and other devices to interpret and present content in a meaningful way. the steps belwo will guider you:

Adding Tags:

- Launch Adobe Acrobat and open the PDF document you want to work on.
- Go to the "View" menu, select "Show/Hide," navigate to "Navigation Panes," and choose "Tags" to open the Tags pane.
- Go to "Tools" > "Accessibility" > "Add Tags to Document" to automatically add tags based on the document's structure. Acrobat will attempt to analyze the content and generate tags accordingly.
- Right-click on an element in your document (e.g., heading, paragraph, image), choose "Properties," and go to the "Tag" tab.
- Click "Add Tags" to create a new tag, and choose the appropriate tag type from the menu.

Tag types:

- Common tag types include Headings (H1, H2, etc.), Paragraphs (P), Tables, Figures, Links, and List Items (LI).

Tagging tables:

- For tables, right-click on the table tag in the Tags pane, select "Properties," and specify header cells and other details.

Tagging images:

- Tag images using the "Figure" tag. Provide alternative text by right-clicking on the image tag, selecting "Properties," and entering descriptive text in the "Alternate Text" field.

Tagging links:

- Ensure that hyperlinks are properly tagged. Right-click on the link, select "Properties," and choose the appropriate tag type.

Editing tags:

- Open the Tags pane if it's not already visible by going to "View" > "Show/Hide" > "Navigation Panes" > "Tags."
- In the Tags pane, find the tag you want to edit. Right-click on the tag and select "Properties."
- In the Properties dialog, you can edit various properties, such as the tag type, title, and attributes. Ensure that the information accurately represents the content.
- To create a logical hierarchy, you can drag and drop tags within the Tags pane. This helps ensure a proper reading order for screen readers.
- Arrange tags in the Tags pane to reflect the correct reading order. This is crucial for users relying on screen readers.
- Use the "Accessibility Checker" under the "Tools" menu to identify and fix tagging issues. The checker will provide feedback on potential accessibility problems.
- After adding or editing tags, save your document to preserve the accessibility improvements.

Using the Tags panel for structure

The Tags panel in Adobe Acrobat is a critical tool for managing the structure of a PDF document, particularly for making it accessible to individuals with disabilities who use screen readers or other assistive technologies. Follow the guide below on how to use the Tags panel for structure in Adobe Acrobat:

- Open your PDF document in Adobe Acrobat.
- Go to the "View" menu, select "Show/Hide," navigate to "Navigation Panes," and choose "Tags" to open the Tags panel.
- If your document is not tagged, you can use the "Add Tags to Document" feature under "Tools" > "Accessibility" to automatically generate tags based on the document's structure.
- Manually tag elements by right-clicking on the element in the document (e.g., text, image, table), selecting "Properties," and assigning the appropriate tag type.

- Common tag types include Headings (H1, H2, etc.), Paragraphs (P), Tables, Figures, Links, and List Items (LI).
- Drag and drop tags within the Tags panel to adjust the document's structure. This helps define the reading order for assistive technologies.
- Arrange tags in the Tags panel to reflect the correct reading order. The order of tags determines how content is presented by screen readers.
- For tables, ensure that each cell is properly tagged. Right-click on the table tag in the Tags panel, select "Properties," and specify header cells and other details.
- Tag images using the "Figure" tag. Provide alternative text by right-clicking on the image tag, selecting "Properties," and entering descriptive text in the "Alternate Text" field.
- Ensure that hyperlinks are properly tagged. Right-click on the link, select "Properties," and choose the appropriate tag type.
- Use the "Accessibility Checker" under the "Tools" menu to identify and fix tagging issues. The checker will provide feedback on potential accessibility problems.
- Specify the document language in the document properties to assist screen readers in proper pronunciation and language-specific processing.
- Tag form fields, buttons, and other interactive elements to ensure they are accessible. Right-click on the interactive element, select "Properties," and choose the appropriate tag type.
- After adding or editing tags, save your document to preserve the accessibility improvements.
- The "Order" panel in Acrobat can be used in conjunction with the Tags panel to refine the reading order of elements.
- Regularly test your document's accessibility using screen readers or other assistive technologies to ensure a positive user experience.

Conducting accessibility checks

Conducting accessibility checks in Adobe Acrobat involves using built-in tools to identify and address potential accessibility issues in your PDF documents. Follow the steps below:

- Open the PDF document you want to check in Adobe Acrobat.
- Go to the "Tools" menu.
- Select "Accessibility."
- Choose "Full Check."
- In the Accessibility Full Check Options dialog, select the accessibility standards you want to check against. Common standards include:
    - WCAG 2.0 (Web Content Accessibility Guidelines): Widely accepted international guidelines.
    - Section 508 (U.S.): U.S. federal standards for electronic and information technology accessibility.
- Click the "Start Checking" button to initiate the accessibility check.
- Acrobat will generate an Accessibility Checker report highlighting any issues found. The report categorizes issues by type (e.g., images, headings, tables).

- Click on each issue to get details and suggestions for fixing the problems.
- For each flagged issue, follow the suggested actions to fix the accessibility problem.
- Common issues may include missing alt text for images, incorrect heading structures, untagged content, and more.
- Use the Tags panel and other editing tools to address identified problems.
- After making changes, you can rerun the accessibility check to ensure that the issues have been resolved.

Running and interpreting accessibility reports

Running an Accessibility Report:

- Open the PDF document you want to check in Adobe Acrobat.
- Go to the "Tools" menu.
- Select "Accessibility."
- Choose "Full Check."
- In the Accessibility Full Check Options dialog, choose the accessibility standards against which you want to check your document (e.g., WCAG 2.0, Section 508).
- Click the "Start Checking" button to initiate the accessibility check.
- After running the accessibility check, Adobe Acrobat will generate a report that lists any issues found in your document. Here's how to interpret the report:
- The Accessibility Checker generates a summary at the top of the report, providing an overview of the number and severity of issues found.
- The report categorizes issues by type (e.g., Images, Headings, Tables). Click on each category to expand and view specific issues.
- Issues are marked with severity icons (e.g., Error, Warning, Information). Clicking on an issue reveals details about the problem and suggested actions.
- Click on each individual issue to get detailed information about the problem, its location in the document, and suggested remediation steps.
- The Accessibility Checker panel on the left provides a summary of the number of issues in each category. Clicking on a category in this panel highlights the related issues in the document.
- Follow the suggested actions to fix each issue. This may involve updating tags, providing alternative text for images, adjusting reading order, and more.
- Use the Tags panel to review and adjust the document's structure, ensuring proper tagging for headings, paragraphs, tables, and other elements.
- Address missing or incorrect alternative text for images by editing the properties of image tags in the Tags panel.
- Use the "Reading Order" tool to visually inspect and adjust the reading order of page elements.
- After making changes, rerun the accessibility check to ensure that issues have been resolved.
- Set document properties, including language and title, in the "File" menu under "Properties."

Testing with Assistive Technologies:

- **Screen readers:** Test your document with popular screen readers (e.g., JAWS, NVDA, VoiceOver) to ensure compatibility and a positive user experience.
- **Other assistive technologies:** Test with screen magnifiers, voice recognition software, and other assistive technologies to cover a broader range of accessibility needs.

Fixing common accessibility issues

This involves addressing problems identified by the Accessibility Checker and making adjustments to ensure that the document is accessible to users with disabilities. learn how to fix some common accessibility issues below:

Missing or Incorrect Alternative Text for Images:

- Open the Tags pane.
- Locate the "Figure" tag associated with the image.
- Right-click on the "Figure" tag and select "Properties."
- Enter descriptive alternative text in the "Alternate Text" field.

Untagged content:

- Open the Tags pane.
- Manually add tags to untagged content by selecting the content, right-clicking, and choosing "Properties."
- In the Properties dialog, navigate to the "Tag" tab and select the appropriate tag type.

Headings structure issues:

- Open the Tags pane.
- Ensure that headings have the correct hierarchy (e.g., H1, H2, etc.).
- Adjust the tag structure by dragging and dropping heading tags within the Tags pane.

Reading order issues:

- Use the "Reading Order" tool under the "Accessibility" menu.
- Visually inspect and adjust the reading order of page elements.
- Make sure the reading order corresponds to the logical order of content.

Table structure issues:

- Open the Tags pane.
- Right-click on the "Table" tag associated with the table.
- Select "Table Editor" to make adjustments to the table structure.

Form field issues:

- Open the Tags pane.
- Tag form fields correctly, using tags such as "Form," "Text," "Check Box," etc.
- Provide descriptive labels for form fields.

Link text issues:

- Open the Tags pane.
- Right-click on the "Link" tag associated with the hyperlink.
- Choose "Properties" and ensure that the link text is descriptive and provides context.

Color and contrast issues

- Ensure sufficient color contrast for text and background.
- Avoid conveying information solely through color; use other visual cues.
- Test color choices using tools or simulations for color blindness.

Document language specification:

- Set the document language in the document properties under the "File" menu.
- This helps screen readers pronounce text correctly and aids in language-specific processing.

Interactive elements accessibility:

- Ensure that interactive elements, such as buttons and links, are keyboard accessible.
- Test navigation using the keyboard to ensure users can interact with these elements.

Advanced form features

Adobe Acrobat provides advanced form features that allow you to create interactive and dynamic PDF forms. These features enable you to design forms with enhanced functionality, such as calculations, validations, and dynamic content. Check below for some advanced form features available in Adobe Acrobat:

Text fields:

- **Multiline text fields:** Create text fields that can accommodate multiple lines of text.
- **Rich text format:** Allow users to format text using different fonts, styles, and sizes within a text field.

Check boxes and radio buttons:

- **Button groups:** Use radio buttons to create exclusive choices within a group, and checkboxes for non-exclusive options.
- **Custom icons:** Customize the appearance of check boxes and radio buttons with custom icons.

Combo boxes and list boxes

- **Combo boxes:** Combine a text field with a drop-down list, allowing users to type or select an option.
- **List boxes:** Create lists with selectable options, including multiple selections.

Buttons:

- **Push buttons:** Create clickable buttons with customizable labels and actions.
- **Submit buttons:** Add buttons that allow users to submit the form data.
- **Reset buttons:** Include buttons to reset form fields to their default values.

Digital signatures:

- **Digital signature fields:** Integrate digital signature fields to enable users to sign forms securely.
- **Certificate-based signatures:** Allow users to sign with digital certificates for added security.

Form field properties:

- **Calculation scripts:** Use JavaScript to perform calculations based on form field values.
- **Validation scripts:** Implement custom validation to ensure data entered meets specified criteria.

Dynamic PDF forms

- **Hide/Show fields:** Use JavaScript to dynamically show or hide form fields based on user input.
- **Conditional formatting:** Apply conditional formatting to form fields based on predefined conditions.

Date and time fields:

- **Date picker:** Include a date picker for users to easily select a date.
- **Time picker:** Add a time picker for selecting a specific time.

Form templates:

- **Create templates:** Design reusable form templates to maintain consistency across multiple documents.
- **Import/Export form data:** Import and export form data between different PDF documents.

Accessibility features:

- **Tagged PDFs:** Ensure your forms are accessible by properly tagging form fields.

- **Read out loud:** Allow users with visual impairments to have form content read aloud.

Chapter 12

Calculations and advanced form field properties

Performing calculations in form fields

The calculation can be done using the built-in JavaScript capabilities.check below for the general guide on how to set up calculations in form fields:

- **Open your PDF form:** Open your PDF form in Adobe Acrobat.
- **Access form editing mode:** Go to "Tools" > "Prepare Form."
- Select the text field where you want the calculation to take place.
- Right-click on the selected text field and choose "Properties."
- In the Properties dialog box, go to the "Calculate" tab.
- If your form has multiple fields with calculations, you might need to set the calculation order. Use the "Calculate" tab to specify the order.
- In the "Calculate" tab, choose the type of calculation you want. For example, you can choose "Value is the" and then specify a custom calculation script.
- In the calculation script editor, you can write JavaScript code to perform the calculation. For example, if you want to add two fields, you can write something like:

Using JavaScript for advanced form calculations

Adobe Acrobat supports JavaScript, and you can use it to perform calculations, validate user input, and manipulate form fields dynamically. Follow the tips below:

Open the JavaScript Console in Adobe Acrobat:

- Open your PDF form in Adobe Acrobat.
- Go to View > Tools > JavaScript > Console.

Accessing Form Fields:

You can access form fields using their names. For example, if you have a text field named "txtField1", you can access it using getField:

Event triggers:

You can trigger calculations based on user actions like field changes or button clicks. For example, to trigger the calculation when the user exits the "num1" or "num2" field, you can use the calculate event:

Custom validation:

You can also add custom validation to ensure that users enter valid data. For example, to ensure that the input is a number:

Adding a button:

You can also add a button that, when clicked, triggers a specific action. For example, a button named "calculateBtn":

Dynamic forms and conditional logic

Creating dynamic forms with conditional logic in Adobe Acrobat using JavaScript allows you to control the visibility, formatting, and behavior of form elements based on user input. Chedck below for an example scenario where you want to show or hide certain fields based on the user's selection:

To create a PDF form with two radio buttons:

- payment Method: User selects the payment method (Credit Card or PayPal).
- creditCardDetails: Additional fields for credit card details, visible only if the user selects "Credit Card."

JavaScript code

- Open the JavaScript Console as mentioned before.
- Access form fields:

Add a custom function to show or hide the credit card details based on the selected payment method:

Add validation to the credit card fields if they are visible:

Creating dynamic forms with show/hide logic

JavaScript Code:

Open the JavaScript Console as mentioned before.

Add a custom function to show or hide the field sets based on the selected category:

Using calculations for conditional form fields

Using calculations for conditional form fields in Adobe Acrobat involves using JavaScript to dynamically set values, perform calculations, or manipulate the appearance of form fields based on user input or other conditions.

"calculateDiscount" function is triggered when the user interacts with the quantity field. The function calculates the "discount" based on the quantity entered and sets the value of the "discount" field accordingly. Additionally, a validation function is attached to the quantity field to ensure that only positive numbers are entered.

Form   data   integration   with   other   applications

Integrating form data from Adobe Acrobat with other applications typically involves using JavaScript to submit the form data to a server or external service. This process can be triggered by events such as form submission, button clicks, or other user interactions. Check below for how you can integrate form data with an external server using the submitForm function:

- If you have a form with fields like name, email, and comments. You want to submit this form data to an external server when the user clicks a "Submit" button.
- Ensure that the URL (submitUrl) is replaced with the actual endpoint where you want to submit the form data.
- Adjust the field names ('name', 'email', 'comments') and form fields (nameField, emailField, commentsField) based on your specific form structure.
- The cSubmitFields parameter in submitForm should contain the form data in the expected format by the server. In this example, it's submitted as a JSON string.
- Depending on your use case, you might need to handle authentication, error handling, or other considerations in your server-side application.

Exporting form data to Excel and other formats

Exporting form data from Adobe Acrobat to Excel or other formats involves using JavaScript to collect the form data and then export it using a suitable method.

In a form with fields like name, email, and comments. You want to export this form data to a CSV file when the user clicks an "Export" button.

- Open the JavaScript Console in Adobe Acrobat.
- Add a custom function to export form data to CSV:
- Adjust the field names ('name', 'email', 'comments') and form fields (nameField, emailField, commentsField) based on your specific form structure.
- The exportToCSV function creates a CSV file with a header row and data row. It then creates a data URI for the CSV content and triggers a download link to save the CSV file.

Integrating form data with external systems

Integrating form data with external systems in Adobe Acrobat often involves submitting form data to a server or API endpoint.

- If you have a PDF form with fields like name, email, and comments. You want to submit this form data to an external server or API endpoint when the user clicks a "Submit" button.

- Open Adobe Acrobat and go to View > Tools > JavaScript > Console.
- Access the form fields using JavaScript.
- Create a custom function that collects form data and submits it to an external server. In this example, we'll use the util.HTTP object for a simple POST request.
- Ensure that you have the correct API endpoint (submitUrl) and that the server expects the data in the specified format. Test the integration in a controlled environment.
- Make sure that the external server or API endpoint supports the method (e.g., POST) and data format (e.g., JSON) that you are using in the script.
- Handle security considerations such as authentication, encryption, and data validation on the server side.
- Depending on your use case, you might need to handle error scenarios, provide feedback to the user, or include additional data in the form submission.

Advanced Security Measures

When working with Adobe Acrobat and handling sensitive information, implementing advanced security measures is crucial to protect the integrity and confidentiality of your documents. Check below for some advanced security measures you can take in Adobe Acrobat:

- **Password protection:** Add a password to restrict access to the document. Users need to enter the password to open the PDF. Set a master password to control permissions such as printing, editing, and extracting text/images.
- **Digital signatures:** Use digital signatures to verify the authenticity and integrity of a document. Signatures can be visible or invisible and can include a timestamp.
- **Certificate security:** Use digital IDs and certificates for secure document signing and encryption. Adobe Acrobat supports various digital ID providers.
- **Encryption:** When creating PDFs, choose strong encryption algorithms (AES 256-bit) to protect the content from unauthorized access.
- JavaScript Security: Disable unnecessary JavaScript actions, especially in forms, to prevent potential security vulnerabilities.
- **Redaction:** Use the redaction tool to permanently remove sensitive content from the document, ensuring it cannot be recovered.
- **Secure document properties:** Remove metadata and hidden information from documents to prevent unintentional data leaks.
- **Document restrictions:** Set document restrictions to control actions such as printing, copying, and modifying content.
- **Security policies:** Define and enforce security policies for document creation, sharing, and distribution within your organization.
- **Secure transmission:** When transmitting sensitive documents, use secure methods such as HTTPS to protect data in transit.
- **Adobe livecycle rights management:** Adobe LiveCycle Rights Management provides advanced document protection and permissions control.

- **Regular software updates:** Keep Adobe Acrobat Updated: Regularly update Adobe Acrobat to ensure you have the latest security patches and features.
- **Document accessibility considerations:** Consider accessibility requirements while implementing security measures to ensure compliance with standards.
- **User education:** Educate users on best practices for secure document handling, password management, and recognizing phishing attempts.
- **Third-party security audits:** Conduct periodic security audits or engage third-party services to assess the security of your PDF documents and workflows.

Chapter 13

Digital signatures and certificates

Creating a Digital Signature:

- Open the PDF document you want to sign in Adobe Acrobat.
- Click on "Tools" in the upper left corner.
- Under "Protect & Standardize," select "Sign & Certify" and then "Place Signature."
- Choose whether you want to type, draw, or use an image of your signature. Follow the on-screen instructions to create or import your signature.
- Once your signature is created, place it on the desired location in the document.
- Save the document to apply the digital signature.

Managing Digital Signatures

- To view existing signatures, go to the "Tools" menu, select "Sign & Certify," and choose "More Sign & Certify" > "Security Settings."
- Right-click on the signature field and select "Properties."
- Go to the "Signature" tab to view details and validation information.
- If you are the document's creator, you can certify it to prevent further changes. Go to "Tools," select "Protect & Standardize," and then "Certify with Visible Signature."
- Under "Security Settings," click on "Add ID" to import or create a digital ID (certificate).
- Under "Security Settings," click on "Manage Trusted Identities" to view and manage the certificates you trust.
- To remove a signature, right-click on the signature field and select "Clear Signature."
- You can add security features to your signature by choosing "Document Security" under "Tools."
- You can add a time stamp to your signature for added validity. Choose "Time Stamp Document" under "Tools."
- Adjust your digital signature preferences by going to "Edit" > "Preferences" > "Signatures."

Validating digital signatures

- Launch Adobe Acrobat and open the PDF document containing the digital signature.
- Click on "View" in the upper menu, then select "Show/Hide" > "Navigation Panes" > "Signatures" to open the Signature panel.
- In the Signature panel, you will see a list of signatures. Click on a signature to view detailed information.
- Check the status of the signature. It should display "Signature is Valid" if the signature is valid. If it's not valid, Adobe Acrobat will provide information about the issue.
- Click on the "Signature Properties" option to access detailed information about the signature. This may include the signer's name, email, time of signing, and other relevant details.

- In the Signature Properties, you can often find an option to view the signer's certificate. Verify that the certificate information is accurate and belongs to a trusted source.
- Ensure that the certificate chain is valid. Check each certificate in the chain to make sure it is not expired and is issued by a trusted Certificate Authority (CA).
- If the signature includes a timestamp, check the timestamp information to ensure that the signature was valid at the time of signing.
- Verify the revocation status of the certificate by checking the Certificate Revocation List (CRL) or using the Online Certificate Status Protocol (OCSP). This information is typically available in the Certificate Viewer.
- Confirm that the document has not been altered since the digital signature was applied. The signature status may indicate if the document has been modified.
- Ensure that the digital ID used to sign the document is from a trusted source. Check your list of trusted identities and certificates in Adobe Acrobat.
- Depending on your version of Adobe Acrobat, you may have additional validation options, such as configuring the level of trust for certificates and setting up automatic signature validation.

Configuring certificate trust settings

- Launch Adobe Acrobat and open the application.
- Go to "Edit" > "Preferences."
- In the Preferences dialog, select "Security (Enhanced)" from the left sidebar.
- Click on "Advanced Preferences" to access more detailed security settings.
- Look for an option related to managing trusted identities or certificates. This might be labeled as "Manage Trusted Identities" or similar.
- In the "Manage Trusted Identities" dialog or a similar section, you can view a list of trusted identities and certificates.
- To add a new trusted root certificate, click on "Add Contact" or a similar option. Then, browse and select the root certificate file (.cer or .crt). After, click "Open" and follow the prompts.
- To remove a trusted identity or certificate, select the item you want to remove then, click on "Remove."
- To adjust trust levels, select the item and click on "Trust Level." Choose the appropriate level of trust.
- To view details, click on an item to view its details. Next, configure Certificate Revocation Settings:
- In the "Security (Enhanced)" preferences, you may find options related to certificate revocation checking. Configure settings based on your security requirements.

Applying and managing security policies

- Launch Adobe Acrobat and open the PDF document you want to apply security policies to.
- Go to "File" > "Properties."
- In the Document Properties dialog, click on the "Security" tab.

You can now choose a security method from the drop-down menu and the common options include:

- **Password security:** Restricts access with a password.
- **Certificate security:** Uses digital certificates for authentication.
- **Adobe LiveCycle rights management:** Controls access and permissions centrally.

Configure security settings by following the tips below:

- Depending on the security method selected, you'll need to configure settings such as password requirements, encryption strength, or certificate options.
- Click "OK" to apply the selected security method and settings.
- Go to "File" > "Properties."
- In the Document Properties dialog, click on the "Security" tab.
- Click on the "Change Settings" button or a similar option.
- Go to "File" > "Properties."
- In the Document Properties dialog, click on the "Security" tab.
- Choose "No Security" or a similar option.
- If password security is applied, you can change the password:
- Go to "File" > "Properties."
- In the Document Properties dialog, click on the "Security" tab.
- Click on the "Change Password" button.
- Go to "File" > "Properties."
- In the Document Properties dialog, click on the "Security" tab.
- View details related to encryption, permissions, and other security features.
- If using Adobe LiveCycle Rights Management, you may need to access additional settings through the LiveCycle server.

Creating and applying security policies

Creating and applying security policies in Adobe Acrobat helps you control access, protect sensitive information, and enforce security measures in your PDF documents. Follow the steps below:

Creating and applying security policies:

- Launch Adobe Acrobat and open the PDF document you want to apply security policies to.

- Go to "File" > "Properties."
- In the Document Properties dialog, click on the "Security" tab.

Choose a security method:

From the Security Method drop-down menu, select the type of security you want to apply. Common options include:

- **Password security:** Restricts access with a password.
- **Certificate security:** Uses digital certificates for authentication.
- **Adobe LiveCycle rights management:** Controls access and permissions centrally.

Configure security settings

- Depending on the selected security method, configure settings such as password requirements, encryption strength, or certificate options.
- Choose "Password Security" from the drop-down.
- Set a password and configure options such as permissions and encryption strength.
- Choose "Certificate Security" from the drop-down.
- Configure options related to digital certificates.
- Choose "Adobe LiveCycle Rights Management" from the drop-down.
- Follow additional steps based on your organization's LiveCycle server setup.

Apply security:

- Click "OK" to apply the selected security method and settings.
- Save the document to apply the security settings.

Managing security policies:

- Go to "File" > "Properties."
- In the Document Properties dialog, click on the "Security" tab.
- Click on the "Change Settings" or "Edit" button.

Remove security:

- Go to "File" > "Properties."
- In the Document Properties dialog, click on the "Security" tab.
- Choose "No Security" or a similar option.

Change password:

- Go to "File" > "Properties."

- In the Document Properties dialog, click on the "Security" tab.
- Click on the "Change Password" button.

View security details:

- Go to "File" > "Properties."
- In the Document Properties dialog, click on the "Security" tab.
- View details related to encryption, permissions, and other security features.

Configuring document restrictions and permissions

- Launch Adobe Acrobat and open the PDF document you want to apply restrictions to.
- Go to "File" > "Properties."
- In the Document Properties dialog, click on the "Security" tab.
- From the Security Method drop-down menu, select "Password Security."
- Enter a password in the "Document Open Password" field. This password is required to open the document.

Configure permissions

Common permissions include:

- **Printing:** Allow or disallow printing of the document.
- **Changes:** Specify what changes can be made, such as filling in form fields or adding comments.
- **Content copying:** Allow or disallow copying text and graphics.
- **Accessibility:** Enable accessibility options for screen readers.

Set Encryption level:

- Choose the encryption level for the document. Higher levels provide stronger security but may limit compatibility with older versions of Acrobat.
- Click "OK" to apply the password security and permissions.
- Save the document to apply the security settings.

Managing document restrictions:

- Go to "File" > "Properties."
- In the Document Properties dialog, click on the "Security" tab.
- Click on the "Change Settings" or "Edit" button.
- If you want to remove restrictions from a PDF document:
- Go to "File" > "Properties."
- In the Document Properties dialog, click on the "Security" tab.
- Choose "No Security" or a similar option.

- If password security is applied, you can change the password:
- Go to "File" > "Properties."
- In the Document Properties dialog, click on the "Security" tab.
- Click on the "Change Password" button.

View document restrictions:

- Go to "File" > "Properties."
- In the Document Properties dialog, click on the "Security" tab.
- View details related to encryption, permissions, and other security features.

Batch processing and automation

Adobe Acrobat provides features for batch processing and automation, allowing users to perform repetitive tasks on multiple PDF files simultaneously. Below are some common tasks and steps for batch processing and automation in Adobe Acrobat:

Combining multiple PDF files:

- Open Adobe Acrobat.
- Go to "File" > "Create" > "Combine Files into a Single PDF."
- Click "Add Files" to select the PDFs you want to combine.
- Arrange files if needed and click "Combine."

Splitting PDF files:

- Open Adobe Acrobat.
- Go to "File" > "Organize Pages" > "Split."
- Choose the method to split (number of pages, file size, bookmarks).
- Configure settings and click "Output Options" if necessary.
- Click "OK" to split the document.

Applying batch sequences:

- Go to "Advanced" > "Document Processing" > "Batch Processing."
- Click "New Sequence" and follow the wizard to set up actions.
- Add actions such as watermarking, headers, or security settings.
- Save the sequence.
- Open Adobe Acrobat.
- Go to "Advanced" > "Document Processing" > "Batch Processing."

- Select the sequence you created and run it on the target files.

Adding watermarks or headers:

- Go to "Tools" > "Edit PDF" > "Watermark" > "Add Watermark."
- Configure settings, select the files, and click "OK."
- Go to "File" > "Document Properties" > "Header & Footer."
- Add headers/footers and choose the pages.
- Click "OK" to apply.

Automating form field recognition:

- Open Adobe Acrobat.
- Go to "File" > "Create" > "PDF Form."
- Acrobat will automatically recognize form fields.

Chapter 14

Automating repetitive tasks with actions

Creating and using batch actions

Creating a Batch Sequence:

- Launch Adobe Acrobat on your computer.
- Go to the "Tools" pane on the right side of the screen.
- Find and open the "Action Wizard" panel.
- Click on "Create New Action" in the Action Wizard panel.
- Choose the individual steps you want your batch action to perform from the available options. Common actions include adding watermarks, merging files, or optimizing PDFs.
- Configure each step according to your requirements. For example, if you're adding watermarks, set the text, font, and position.
- Click on "Add Files" to include the PDF files on which you want to perform the batch action. You can select individual files or an entire folder.
- Give your batch action a meaningful name and click "Save." This ensures that you can reuse this sequence in the future.

Running a Batch Process

- Open the "Action Wizard" panel.
- Under "Available Actions," choose the batch action you created.
- Indicate whether you want to process all files in a specific folder, all open files, or a selection of files.
- Define where the processed files should be saved and whether the original files should be replaced or saved in a different location.
- Click "Next" and then "Save" to start the batch process. Acrobat will perform the specified actions on the selected files.
- After the batch process completes, review the processed files to ensure that the actions were executed correctly.

Tips and best practices:

- Before running a batch process on a large number of files, test it on a small batch to ensure that the actions are working as expected.
- If the batch process involves modifying files, consider making a backup of the original files before running the action.
- Familiarize yourself with the available action steps and their settings to create effective batch sequences.
- Periodically review and update your batch actions as your needs change. You can modify existing actions or create new ones.
- Adobe Acrobat offers a variety of built-in actions, and you can also create custom JavaScript-based actions for more advanced tasks.

Common batch processing scenarios

- **Watermarking multiple PDFs:** Add a watermark, such as a company logo or a "Draft" stamp, to a batch of PDF files.
- **Merging PDF files:** Combine multiple PDFs into a single document, useful for assembling reports or presentations.
- **Splitting PDFs:** Divide large PDF files into smaller ones based on specific criteria, such as a certain number of pages or bookmarks.
- **Page numbering:** Add page numbers to PDF files, helping with document organization and navigation.
- **Text Search and replace:** Search for specific text or phrases in multiple PDF files and replace them with updated content.
- **Optimizing PDFs:** Compress images, reduce file size, and optimize PDFs for web or email distribution.
- **Securing PDFs:** Apply password protection, encryption, or other security measures to a batch of PDF files.
- **Converting File formats:** Convert multiple files from one format (e.g., Word or Excel) to PDF or vice versa.
- **OCR (Optical Character Recognition):** Perform OCR on scanned PDFs to make the text searchable and selectable.
- **Redaction:** Automatically redact sensitive information, such as personal data or confidential details, across multiple PDF files.
- **Form field creation:** Add form fields to PDFs in bulk, making them fillable for users.
- **Metadata editing:** Modify metadata information, such as author, title, and keywords, for a batch of PDF documents.
- **Annotation and commenting:** Apply annotations, comments, or markup to multiple PDF files simultaneously.
- **Applying color profiles:** Ensure consistent color profiles across a batch of PDF files for printing or digital display.
- **Booklet Printing:** Rearrange pages and format PDFs for booklet-style printing.
- **Stamping Confidential or Draft Labels:** Automatically apply stamps indicating document status, like "Confidential" or "Draft."
- **Extracting Images or Text:** Extract images or text content from a batch of PDF files for reuse or analysis.
- **Embedding Fonts:** Ensure that fonts are embedded in PDFs for consistent display across different devices.
- **Flattening Annotations and Form Fields:** Flatten annotations and form fields to make them part of the PDF content, preventing further edits.
- **Converting Color to Grayscale:** Convert color PDFs to grayscale for printing or to reduce file size.

Creating and running batch sequences

Creating a Batch Sequence:

- Launch Adobe Acrobat on your computer.
- Go to the "Tools" pane on the right side of the screen.
- Find and open the "Action Wizard" panel.
- Click on "Create New Action" in the Action Wizard panel.
- Choose the individual steps you want your batch action to perform from the available options. These could include tasks like adding watermarks, merging files, or optimizing PDFs.
- For each selected step, configure the settings according to your requirements. For example, if you're adding watermarks, set the text, font, and position.
- Click on "Add Files" to include the PDF files on which you want to perform the batch action. You can select individual files or an entire folder.
- Specify where the processed files should be saved and whether the original files should be replaced or saved in a different location.
- Give your batch action a meaningful name and click "Save." This ensures that you can reuse this sequence in the future.

Running a batch process:

- Open the "Action Wizard" panel.
- Under "Available Actions," choose the batch action you created.
- Indicate whether you want to process all files in a specific folder, all open files, or a selection of files.
- Click "Next" and then "Save" to start the batch process. Acrobat will perform the specified actions on the selected files.
- After the batch process completes, review the processed files to ensure that the actions were executed correctly.

Tips and best practices:

- Before running a batch process on a large number of files, test it on a small batch to ensure that the actions are working as expected.
- If the batch process involves modifying files, consider making a backup of the original files before running the action.
- Familiarize yourself with the available action steps and their settings to create effective batch sequences.
- Periodically review and update your batch actions as your needs change. You can modify existing actions or create new ones.
- Adobe Acrobat offers a variety of built-in actions, and you can also create custom JavaScript-based actions for more advanced tasks.

Organizing and managing batch sequences

Organizing batch sequences:

- Group your batch sequences based on their types or purposes. For example, you might have folders for watermarking, merging, or optimizing sequences.
- Give each batch sequence a clear and descriptive name. This makes it easier to identify the purpose of the sequence at a glance.
- Assign colors or categories to your batch sequences to visually distinguish between different types of actions. This can be especially helpful when you have a variety of sequences.
- Within the Action Wizard, you can add comments or descriptions to each step of your batch sequence. This documentation helps you understand the purpose of each step, making it easier to modify or update sequences later.
- Organize your sequences in a logical order. You can sort them alphabetically or arrange them based on priority or frequency of use.

Managing batch sequences:

- Periodically review your batch sequences to ensure they are still relevant and meet your current workflow requirements. Update sequences as needed.
- Export and save your batch sequences to a secure location. This ensures that you have a backup in case of software updates, reinstallation, or system changes.
- If you are working in a collaborative environment, share your batch sequences with team members. This ensures consistency in workflows and helps others benefit from your predefined actions.
- Create a document or spreadsheet that outlines the purpose and use case of each batch sequence. This documentation can be valuable for training purposes or when sharing workflows with others.
- Before running a batch sequence on a large set of files, test it on a small sample to ensure that the sequence performs as expected. This helps avoid unintended consequences.
- Explore the possibility of creating custom JavaScript-based actions for advanced or unique tasks. This allows you to tailor batch sequences to specific needs.
- Leverage features within the Action Wizard, such as the ability to edit, delete, or duplicate existing sequences. This flexibility is helpful when refining your batch processes.
- Depending on your workflow requirements, consider exploring third-party plugins or scripts that can extend the functionality of Adobe Acrobat's Action Wizard.

Running batch sequences for efficiency

Running batch sequences in Adobe Acrobat efficiently involves optimizing your workflows to save time and reduce manual effort. This tips below will guide you on how to achieve efficiency when using batch sequences:

- Before creating batch sequences, carefully plan your workflow and identify repetitive tasks that can be automated. Customize your batch sequences to suit your specific needs.

- Design batch sequences that are versatile and can be reused for various types of PDF files. This helps save time by not having to recreate sequences for similar tasks.
- Organize your batch sequences based on priority or frequency of use. This ensures that frequently used sequences are easily accessible and saves time searching for them.
- Streamline your batch sequences by eliminating unnecessary steps. Focus on the essential actions that contribute to your workflow efficiency.
- Take advantage of presets and default settings within your batch sequences. This minimizes the need for manual input, saving time and reducing the chance of errors.
- Explore automation features such as JavaScript scripting to extend the capabilities of your batch sequences. This allows for more advanced and customized actions.
- Before applying batch sequences to a large set of files, test them on a small sample to ensure they work as intended. This prevents potential errors and the need for rework.
- Adobe Acrobat supports watched folders, where sequences can be automatically applied to files added to a specified folder. This is useful for ongoing or repetitive tasks.
- Schedule batch processing during off-peak times to avoid conflicts with other tasks. This ensures that your computer's resources are dedicated to running sequences efficiently.
- Configure your batch sequences to optimize PDF settings, such as reducing file size without compromising quality. This is particularly useful when dealing with large numbers of documents.
- Keep an eye on the progress of your batch sequences, especially for resource-intensive tasks. Monitoring allows you to address any issues promptly.
- Include error-checking mechanisms in your batch sequences. This helps identify and address issues, preventing the need to rerun sequences due to errors.
- Create specialized batch sequences for specific tasks, such as watermarking, merging, or OCR. This allows you to choose the most relevant sequence for the job at hand.
- Document your batch sequences and provide training materials for team members. This ensures that everyone follows standardized procedures, promoting efficiency across the team.
- Periodically review and update your batch sequences to align with any changes in your workflow or software updates. This ensures continued efficiency.

Using the Action Wizard

The Action Wizard in Adobe Acrobat is a powerful tool that allows you to automate a series of tasks, creating custom sequences to process PDF files more efficiently. The step below will guide you on how to use the Action Wizard:

- Launch Adobe Acrobat on your computer.
- Go to the "Tools" pane on the right side of the screen.
- In older versions, you may find the Action Wizard under the "View" > "Tools" menu.
- Click on "Action Wizard" to open the panel.
- In the Action Wizard panel, click on "Create New Action."

- In the "Add Action" dialog, choose the specific actions you want to include in your sequence. These actions can range from simple tasks like adding watermarks to more complex ones like combining files.
- For each selected action step, configure the settings according to your requirements. This may involve specifying text for a watermark, setting compression options, or defining security settings.
- Click on the "Add Files" button to include the PDF files you want to process with the batch sequence. You can add individual files, entire folders, or use files that are currently open.
- Specify where the processed files should be saved. You can overwrite the original files, save them in a different location, or create a new set of files.
- Give your action a meaningful name in the "Save Action" dialog, and click "Save." This ensures you can reuse the sequence in the future.
- Once your action is saved, select it in the Action Wizard panel.
- Click on "Next" to review the sequence, then click "Save" to run the batch process.
- Acrobat will process the selected files according to the defined sequence of actions.
- After the batch process is complete, review the processed files to ensure that the actions were executed correctly.

Overview of the Action Wizard

The Action Wizard in Adobe Acrobat is a robust tool that allows users to automate repetitive tasks by creating custom sequences of actions. These actions can range from simple operations like adding watermarks to more complex processes like combining, optimizing, or securing PDF files. check below for some of the main features:

- **Accessing the action Wizard:** The Action Wizard is accessible from the "Tools" pane on the right side of the Adobe Acrobat interface.
- **Creating a new action:** Users can create a new action by selecting "Action Wizard" and choosing "Create New Action." This opens a dialog where you can define the sequence of actions to be performed.
- **Selecting action steps:** The Action Wizard allows users to choose from a variety of predefined actions. These can include tasks like adding watermarks, resizing pages, merging files, and more.
- **Configuring action settings:** Once actions are selected, users can configure specific settings for each action step. This may involve setting text for watermarks, adjusting compression settings, or defining security parameters.
- **Adding files:** Users can specify the PDF files on which the action sequence will be applied. Files can be added individually, from a folder, or by using currently open files.
- **Setting output options:** Users can define where the processed files should be saved. This can include overwriting the original files, saving them in a different location, or creating a new set of files.
- **Saving the action:** After configuring the action steps, users can save the action with a meaningful name for future use.

- **Running the batch process:** Once the action is saved, users can select it in the Action Wizard panel and proceed to run the batch process. The selected actions will be applied to the specified PDF files.
- **Reviewing processed files:** Users can review the processed files to ensure that the actions were executed correctly and that the desired changes have been applied.
- **Editing or deleting actions:** The Action Wizard panel allows users to edit or delete existing actions. This provides flexibility for refining or updating sequences based on changing requirements.
- **Combining multiple actions:** Users can create more complex sequences by combining multiple actions within a single sequence. For example, one can add a watermark and then merge files in a single action.
- **JavaScript actions:** For advanced users, the Action Wizard supports the inclusion of JavaScript-based actions, allowing for highly customized and intricate tasks.
- **Built-In actions:** Adobe Acrobat comes with a set of built-in actions that serve as templates or starting points for common tasks. These can be customized to suit specific needs.
- **Documentation and help:** Adobe provides documentation and help resources for users to understand and effectively use the Action Wizard. This includes information on built-in actions and JavaScript scripting.

Creating and sharing custom wizards

Creating Custom Action Sequences:

- Launch Adobe Acrobat on your computer.
- Go to the "Tools" pane on the right side of the screen.
- Find and open the "Action Wizard" panel.
- Click on "Create New Action" in the Action Wizard panel.
- Choose the individual steps you want your custom action to perform from the available options. These actions can include tasks like adding watermarks, merging files, or optimizing PDFs.
- For each selected step, configure the settings according to your requirements. Set text for watermarks, adjust compression settings, or define security parameters.
- Give your custom action a meaningful name and click "Save." This ensures that you can reuse this sequence in the future.

Running a Custom Action Sequence:

- Open the "Action Wizard" panel.
- Under "Available Actions," choose the custom action you created.
- Click on "Add Files" to include the PDF files on which you want to perform the custom action. You can select individual files or an entire folder.
- Specify where the processed files should be saved and whether the original files should be replaced or saved in a different location.

- Click "Next" and then "Save" to start the custom action process. Acrobat will perform the specified actions on the selected files.
- Create a document (Word, PDF, or another format) that outlines the steps involved in creating the custom action. Include details on each action, such as settings and configurations.
- Share the document with others who might need to replicate the custom action sequence. You can use email, shared folders, or collaboration platforms.
- Provide clear instructions so that others can recreate the custom action in their own Adobe Acrobat instances. This might involve detailed explanations, screenshots, or step-by-step guides.

Advanced Collaboration Features

Adobe Acrobat offers several advanced collaboration features that facilitate team collaboration, document review, and feedback collection. These features help streamline workflows and enhance communication among team members working on PDF documents. Check below for some of the advanced collaboration features in Adobe Acrobat:

Shared reviews: Shared Reviews enable multiple users to review and comment on a PDF document simultaneously. The comments and annotations are centrally collected, making it easier to manage feedback. Initiate a shared review by selecting "Review" > "Share for Review." Share the document via email or a cloud storage service. Reviewers can add comments, annotations, and markups in real-time.

Commenting and markup tools: Adobe Acrobat provides a variety of commenting and markup tools for collaborative document review. Users can add comments, highlight text, draw shapes, and attach files. Access the commenting tools from the "Comment" pane on the right side of the screen. Use the various tools to add comments, annotations, and markups to the document.

Form field collaboration: Collaborate on fillable forms by sharing form field data with other users. This feature is especially useful for collecting data and feedback from multiple contributors. Create a fillable form using form fields. Share the form, and when recipients fill in the form, the data can be collected and merged into a single document.

Integration with Adobe sign: Adobe Acrobat integrates with Adobe Sign, allowing users to send documents for e-signatures. This is crucial for collaborative workflows that involve document approvals and signatures. Initiate the e-signature process by selecting "Tools" > "Adobe Sign." Follow the prompts to send the document for signatures.

Real-time Collaboration (Adobe LiveCycle Collaboration Service): Real-time collaboration enables multiple users to collaborate on a document in real-time. Changes made by one user are instantly visible to others. As of my last update, real-time collaboration may require Adobe LiveCycle Collaboration Service, and access to this service may depend on your Adobe Acrobat subscription.

Version control and document history: Track changes and versions of a document to manage collaborative edits. Document history helps users review changes and revert to previous versions if needed. Access version control and document history features through the "File" menu or document properties.

Security and permissions:

Set document permissions to control who can view, edit, or comment on a PDF. Password protect documents, apply encryption, and control access to sensitive information. Access security and permissions settings through the "File" menu or document properties.

Review tracker: The Review Tracker helps users keep track of comments and annotations made by multiple reviewers. It provides an organized summary of feedback. Access the Review Tracker from the "Comment" pane to see a summary of all comments, filter by reviewer, and manage feedback efficiently.

Mobile collaboration: Collaborate on PDF documents using mobile devices. Users can review, comment, and markup documents on the go. Install the Adobe Acrobat mobile app on your iOS or Android device. Open a document and use the commenting tools to collaborate.

Chapter 15

Shared reviews and comment tracking

Initiating and managing shared reviews

Initiating a Shared Review:

- Launch Adobe Acrobat and open the PDF document you want to share for review.
- In Adobe Acrobat, go to the "Review" tab, located in the top menu bar.
- Click on the "Share for Review" option. This might be labeled differently in older versions of Acrobat.
- Choose the preferred method for sharing the document. Options may include email, a shared network location, or a cloud storage service. Follow the on-screen prompts to complete the setup.
- Configure reviewer options, such as allowing reviewers to see each other's comments, requiring a login, or setting a deadline for the review.
- Enter the email addresses of the reviewers or choose a shared location. Send invitations to the selected reviewers to participate in the shared review.
- Reviewers will receive invitations containing a link to the shared document. They can open the document in their own Acrobat instances to start the review.

Managing a shared review:

- As the initiator, access the "Review Tracker" from the "Review" tab or the "Comments" pane. This provides an overview of comments, statuses, and deadlines.
- Use the Review Tracker to monitor the progress of the review. Track who has completed their review, view their comments, and manage the overall review status.
- As reviewers submit comments and feedback, you can collect and apply the feedback using the "Collect Feedback" button in the Review Tracker.
- If a deadline was set during the initiation, monitor the deadline status in the Review Tracker. You may send reminders to reviewers as the deadline approaches.
- Filter comments in the "Comments" pane based on reviewer, status, or type of comment. This helps in organizing and addressing specific feedback.
- Once the review is complete, close the shared review using the "Close Review" option in the Review Tracker. This finalizes the review process.
- Reviewers can see each other's comments, facilitating collaboration. The comments are centralized in the PDF document, making it easy to manage and address feedback.
- Even after the review is closed, historical data is retained, allowing you to access comments and feedback for future reference.

Tracking and resolving comments in shared reviews

Tracking and resolving comments in shared reviews within Adobe Acrobat involves using the Comment pane and Review Tracker. The steps below will guide you on how to track, manage, and resolve comments during a shared review:

Tracking comments:

- Launch Adobe Acrobat and open the PDF document that is part of the shared review.
- Go to the "Comment" pane on the right side of the screen. This pane displays all comments, annotations, and markups made by reviewers.
- In the "Comments" pane, you can see a list of all comments organized by reviewer. Clicking on a comment highlights the corresponding area in the document.
- Use the filtering options in the "Comments" pane to filter comments by reviewer, status, or type of comment. This helps in organizing and focusing on specific feedback.

Resolving comments:

- To respond to a comment, select the comment in the "Comments" pane. A text box appears where you can type your response. Click "Reply" to add your response.
- After addressing a comment, you can mark it as resolved. Right-click on the comment in the "Comments" pane and choose "Resolve." The resolved comment is visually distinguished from unresolved comments.
- Use the "Show Resolved Comments" option in the "Comments" pane to view previously resolved comments. This allows you to see the history of the comments and resolutions.
- If necessary, you can unresolve a comment. Right-click on the resolved comment and choose "Unresolve." This action makes the comment active again.

Using the review tracker

- Go to the "Review" tab and click on "Review Tracker." This tool provides an overview of the review process, including reviewer statuses and comments.
- In the Review Tracker, you can monitor the progress of each reviewer. It shows whether reviewers have started, completed, or not yet participated in the review.
- Use the "Collect Feedback" option in the Review Tracker to gather all the comments from reviewers. This is particularly useful when you want to compile feedback into a single document.
- If a deadline was set during the shared review initiation, the Review Tracker helps you monitor the deadline status and send reminders to reviewers if needed.

Closing the Shared Review:

- Once the shared review is complete and you have addressed all comments, you can close the review. Use the "Close Review" option in the Review Tracker.

- Before closing the review, you can save a summary of comments. This document includes all comments, resolved or unresolved, and provides a record of the review.
- Even after closing the review, historical data is retained, allowing you to access comments and feedback for future reference.

Collaborating in real-time with shared reviews

Collaborating in real-time with shared reviews in Adobe Acrobat involves using the shared review feature, allowing multiple users to simultaneously review and comment on a PDF document. Check below for tips on how to collaborate in real-time using shared reviews:

Initiating a real-time shared review:

- Launch Adobe Acrobat and open the PDF document you want to share for a real-time review.
- In Adobe Acrobat, go to the "Review" tab, located in the top menu bar.
- Click on the "Share for Review" option. This might be labeled differently in older versions of Acrobat.
- Choose the option for real-time review or collaboration. Follow the on-screen prompts to set up the real-time review.
- Enter the email addresses of the reviewers or choose a shared location. Send invitations to the selected reviewers to join the real-time review.
- Reviewers will receive invitations containing a link to the shared document. They can open the document in their own Acrobat instances to start the real-time review.

Collaborating in real-time:

- As reviewers make comments, annotations, or markups in the document, these changes are visible to all participants in real-time. Each reviewer can see the comments made by others.
- Utilize communication tools within Adobe Acrobat, such as chat or messaging, to facilitate real-time communication between reviewers. This is especially useful for discussing specific points or addressing questions.
- Some versions of Adobe Acrobat support live annotations, allowing reviewers to see each other's annotations as they are being made. Check your specific version for this feature.

Tracking and managing real-time comments:

- Go to the "Comment" pane on the right side of the screen. This pane displays all comments, annotations, and markups made by reviewers in real-time.
- In the "Comments" pane, you can see a live feed of comments organized by reviewer. Clicking on a comment highlights the corresponding area in the document.
- If resolving comments is part of your collaboration, you can do so in real-time. Right-click on a comment in the "Comments" pane and choose "Resolve." The resolved status is instantly visible to all participants.

- Use the filtering options in the "Comments" pane to filter comments by reviewer, status, or type of comment. This helps in organizing and focusing on specific feedback as it happens.

Closing the real-time shared review:

- Once the real-time review is complete, you can end the session. This typically involves closing the shared review or stopping the real-time collaboration features.
- Before ending the review, you can save a summary of comments. This document includes all comments, resolved or unresolved, and provides a record of the real-time review.

Real-time collaboration features and benefits

Adobe Acrobat provides real-time collaboration features that enable users to work together on PDF documents simultaneously. These features enhance communication, streamline workflows, and facilitate more efficient collaboration among team members. Check below for some key real-time collaboration features and their benefits in Adobe Acrobat:

Real-time collaboration features:

Shared Reviews allow multiple users to review and comment on a PDF document at the same time. Comments and annotations are centrally collected, providing a collaborative environment. Multiple reviewers can provide feedback in real-time and all comments are stored in one place, simplifying the review process.

Live Annotations:

Live annotations enable users to see each other's annotations as they are being made. This is particularly useful for collaborative discussions and immediate feedback. Annotations are visible to all participants as they are created and enables real-time discussions around specific points in the document.

Real-time chat and messaging:

Adobe Acrobat may include real-time chat or messaging features, allowing users to communicate with each other directly within the application. Team members can communicate without leaving the application and users can quickly address questions or seek clarification.

Shared workspace

Some versions of Adobe Acrobat may offer a shared workspace, providing a centralized location for collaboration, file sharing, and discussions. All collaboration-related activities are consolidated in one place and simplifies the process of sharing documents and resources.

Best practices for real-time collaboration

Real-time collaboration in Adobe Acrobat can greatly enhance team workflows and streamline the document review process. To ensure a smooth and effective collaborative experience, consider the following best practices:

Before collaborating:

- **Choose the right collaboration method:** Understand the available collaboration features in your version of Adobe Acrobat. Choose the method that best suits your team's needs, whether it's a shared review, live annotations, or real-time chat.
- **Ensure everyone has access:** Confirm that all team members have access to Adobe Acrobat and are using a compatible version. This helps avoid compatibility issues during the collaboration process.
- **Define collaboration guidelines:** Establish clear guidelines for collaboration, including expectations for feedback, communication, and document updates. Ensure that all team members are familiar with the collaboration tools.

Initiating Collaboration:

- **Set up shared reviews carefully:** If using shared reviews, take the time to set up the review carefully. Define reviewer roles, permissions, and deadlines. Clearly communicate the purpose of the review to participants.
- **Provide clear instructions:** Clearly instruct participants on how to access and use the collaboration features. Provide guidelines for commenting, resolving issues, and using communication tools.
- **Communicate expectations:** Clearly communicate the expectations for collaboration, including the timeframe for feedback and any specific areas that require attention. This helps keep the collaboration focused and productive.

During Collaboration:

- Regularly check the progress of the collaboration using tools like the Review Tracker. This allows you to see who has participated, who has completed their review, and whether any issues need attention.
- Encourage all team members to actively participate in the collaboration process. This includes providing feedback, making annotations, and engaging in real-time discussions.
- If available, use real-time communication features, such as live chat or messaging within Adobe Acrobat. This facilitates immediate communication and helps address questions or concerns promptly.

Managing Comments and Annotations:

- If your collaboration involves resolving comments, address and resolve them promptly. This helps in maintaining an organized and resolved comment status.
- Clearly document any changes made during the collaboration. If live annotations are used, make sure team members are aware of the changes being made in real-time.

After Collaboration:

- After the collaboration is complete, use tools like "Collect Feedback" to gather all comments and create a summary document. This document serves as a comprehensive record of the collaboration.
- If applicable, formally close the collaboration session or shared review. This indicates that the collaborative phase is complete, and the document is ready for the next steps.
- Encourage team members to provide feedback on the collaboration process. This can help identify areas for improvement in future collaborations.

General collaboration tips:

- If the document contains sensitive information, ensure that appropriate security measures, such as password protection, are in place.
- Keep Adobe Acrobat updated to the latest version to access new features, improvements, and bug fixes related to collaboration.
- Provide training or access to support resources for team members who may be new to Adobe Acrobat or its collaboration features.
- Clearly label document versions to avoid confusion. If changes are substantial, consider creating a new version of the document.

Managing review cycles

Managing review cycles in Adobe Acrobat involves overseeing the process of document review, collecting feedback from reviewers, addressing comments, and ensuring a smooth collaboration workflow. Check below for steps and best practices for managing review cycles in Adobe Acrobat:

Before starting the review:

- Ensure that the document is properly prepared and ready for review. This includes addressing any formatting issues, checking for completeness, and providing clear instructions to reviewers.
- Clearly define who the reviewers are and their specific roles in the review process. Designate roles such as primary reviewer, secondary reviewer, and approver if necessary.
- Clearly communicate the objectives of the review. Specify the aspects that require attention, such as content accuracy, formatting, or compliance with guidelines.

Initiating the review:

- Consider using Adobe Acrobat's shared review feature for a collaborative and centralized review process. Shared reviews enable multiple users to comment and provide feedback on the same document.
- Establish review deadlines to ensure a timely and efficient process. Clearly communicate the deadlines to reviewers, allowing them adequate time to provide thoughtful feedback.
- Offer guidelines to reviewers on how to use commenting tools, how to highlight issues, and any specific areas that require attention. This helps standardize the feedback process.

During the review:

- Regularly check the progress of the review using Adobe Acrobat's Review Tracker or similar tools. Monitor which reviewers have participated, who has completed their review, and the overall status of the review.
- Encourage collaboration among reviewers, especially if using shared reviews. Allow them to see each other's comments, fostering discussion and ensuring that all perspectives are considered.
- If urgent issues arise during the review, address them promptly. Use real-time communication features or direct communication channels to resolve critical matters.

Advanced review management strategies

Advanced review management strategies in Adobe Acrobat involve leveraging the software's features to streamline collaboration, manage feedback effectively, and ensure a smooth review process. Here are advanced strategies to enhance your review management in Adobe Acrobat:

- **Custom review workflows:** Design custom review workflows based on the complexity of your document review process. This may involve defining different stages, assigning specific roles to reviewers, and establishing a clear sequence of tasks.
- **Automated review processes:** Explore the use of scripts or automation tools to streamline repetitive tasks in the review process. Automation can help in collecting feedback, summarizing comments, or applying standardized annotations.
- **Review tracker customization:** Customize the Review Tracker in Adobe Acrobat to fit your specific needs. Use filters, sorting options, and custom fields to organize and track the progress of reviews more efficiently.
- **Conditional reviews:** Implement conditional reviews based on specific criteria. For instance, certain sections of a document may require review only if changes have been made in those areas. Conditional reviews help in focusing attention where it is needed.
- **Integration with document management systems:** Integrate Adobe Acrobat with document management systems to enhance version control, access control, and document retrieval. This ensures that reviewers are working with the latest version of the document.
- **Security measures:** Implement advanced security measures for sensitive documents. Utilize encryption, password protection, and other security features to safeguard the document during the review process.
- **Real-time collaboration with external stakeholders:** Explore ways to collaborate in real-time with external stakeholders who may not have Adobe Acrobat. Utilize tools like Adobe Document Cloud or shared cloud storage solutions for seamless collaboration.

Resolving conflicts and discrepancies

Resolving conflicts and discrepancies in Adobe Acrobat during the review process is crucial to maintaining document accuracy and ensuring that feedback is properly addressed. Follow the steps below on to effectively resolve conflicts and discrepancies:

- Thoroughly review all comments and annotations made by different reviewers. Identify any conflicting feedback or discrepancies in the comments, suggestions, or changes proposed by reviewers.
- Prioritize conflicts based on their impact on the document. Focus on resolving critical conflicts that may affect the document's accuracy, clarity, or compliance.
- Encourage communication between reviewers to discuss conflicting comments. Provide a platform for reviewers to clarify their feedback and understand each other's perspectives.
- Leverage the comment status feature in Adobe Acrobat to track the status of each comment. Ensure that comments are appropriately marked as resolved, unresolved, or in progress.
- Use tools like the "Collect Feedback" feature in Adobe Acrobat to consolidate all comments into a single document. This helps in reviewing and addressing conflicts in a centralized manner.
- Ensure that all reviewers are working with the latest version of the document. Clear version control helps in avoiding conflicts arising from discrepancies between different document versions.
- Establish clear guidelines for the review process, including instructions on providing feedback and resolving conflicts. Share these guidelines with reviewers to set expectations.
- When conflicts arise, encourage reviewers to work together to find a resolution. This collaborative approach fosters teamwork and ensures that diverse perspectives are considered.
- If conflicts persist, consider holding review meetings to discuss and address discrepancies. Real-time discussions can lead to quicker resolutions and a shared understanding among reviewers.

Customizing Adobe Acrobat

Customizing Adobe Acrobat allows you to tailor the software to your specific needs and preferences. Check below for the various customization options and steps you can take to personalize your Adobe Acrobat experience:

Toolbars and panels:

- **Customize toolbars:** Right-click on the toolbar area and choose "Customize Quick Tools." Drag and drop tools to customize the toolbar with frequently used features.
- **Show/Hide panels:** Use the "View" menu to show or hide various panels such as the Tools, Comment, and Navigation panels.

Preferences:

- **Access preferences:** Go to "Edit" > "Preferences" (Windows) or "Acrobat" > "Preferences" (Mac) to access preferences.
- **General preferences:** Customize settings related to default view, behavior, and interface options.
- **Commenting preferences:** Adjust settings related to commenting and annotation tools.
- **Document properties:** Modify settings for how documents are displayed, printed, and handled.

Custom stamps:

- Design and use custom stamps for annotations. You can create stamps for signatures, approval, or other frequently used markings.

Custom tools:

- Use the "Customize Quick Tools" option to create custom tools that suit your specific workflow.

Keyboard shortcuts

- Customize keyboard shortcuts for various commands by going to "Edit" > "Preferences" > "General" > "Edit Custom Shortcuts."

Custom page display:

- Customize how pages are displayed by going to "View" > "Page Display" and choosing options like single page, continuous scroll, or two-page view.

Themes and skins:

- Some versions of Adobe Acrobat allow you to change the interface theme. Look for options related to themes or skins in the preferences.

Workspaces:

- Arrange panels and tools to create a custom workspace. Save it for easy access using the "View" > "Workspaces" menu.

Custom profiles:

- Create Custom Profiles: If you frequently work with specific document settings, create custom profiles. Go to "Edit" > "Preferences" > "Document Processing" > "Optimize Scanned PDF" to create and manage profiles.

Chapter 16

Custom toolsets and quick tools

Creating and organizing custom toolsets

Creating and organizing custom toolsets in Adobe Acrobat allows you to streamline your workflow by grouping frequently used tools together for quick access. Here's a step-by-step guide on how to create and organize custom toolsets in Adobe Acrobat:

Creating a custom toolset

- Launch Adobe Acrobat on your computer.
- Click on the "Tools" tab in the upper left corner to open the Tools pane.
- In the Tools pane, locate and click on the "More Tools" option (usually represented by three dots or a gear icon). This opens the Custom Tools pane.
- In the Custom Tools pane, click on the "Create a new toolset" icon (usually a folder icon or a plus sign). This action prompts you to enter a name for your new toolset.
- Enter a descriptive name for your toolset and click "OK" or "Create." This will create a new, empty toolset.
- To add tools to your toolset, click on the "Add a tool" icon within the toolset. This will open a menu where you can select tools from various categories, such as Commenting, Editing, or Forms.
- After selecting a tool, drag and drop it into your custom toolset. Repeat this process for each tool you want to include in the toolset.
- To organize your toolset, you can rearrange the order of tools by dragging and dropping them within the toolset. Place frequently used tools at the top for quick access.

Accessing and using custom toolsets

- In the Tools pane, use the drop-down menu to switch to your custom toolset. This displays the tools you've added in a convenient, organized manner.
- Click on the desired tool within your custom toolset to activate it. This allows you to use the selected tool for various actions, such as commenting, editing, or form creation.

Editing or Deleting Custom Toolsets:

- To edit a custom toolset, click on the gear icon next to the toolset name in the Custom Tools pane. This opens a menu where you can rename, add, or remove tools.
- If you want to delete a custom toolset, click on the gear icon next to the toolset name and select the "Delete" option. Confirm the deletion when prompted.

Configuring quick tools for efficiency

Configuring Quick Tools in Adobe Acrobat is an excellent way to streamline your workflow by providing easy access to frequently used tools. Quick Tools allow you to create a customized toolbar with shortcuts to specific tools and features that you use regularly. Follow the steps below:

- Launch Adobe Acrobat on your computer.
- Click on the "Tools" tab in the upper-left corner to open the Tools pane.
- In the Tools pane, you'll find the "Quick Tools" section. If you don't see it, click on the "More Tools" option (usually represented by three dots or a gear icon) to access additional tool options.
- To customize Quick Tools, click on the "Customize Quick Tools" icon within the Quick Tools section. This icon is often represented by a pencil or an "Edit" button.
- In the Customize Quick Tools dialog, you'll see a list of available tools on the left and your Quick Tools on the right. Drag and drop tools from the left to the right to add them to your Quick Tools.
- Arrange the tools in the Quick Tools bar in the order you prefer. Drag and drop to reposition the tools based on your workflow and frequency of use.
- To remove a tool from the Quick Tools bar, simply drag it back to the list on the left. Alternatively, right-click on a tool in the Quick Tools bar and select "Remove from Quick Tools."
- For even quicker access, you can assign keyboard shortcuts to specific tools. Click on the gear icon in the Customize Quick Tools dialog and select "Edit Shortcuts." Assign a keyboard shortcut to each tool as needed.

Once you've configured your Quick Tools to your satisfaction, click "OK" or "Save" to apply the changes and close the Customize Quick Tools dialog.

Creating and using custom stamps

Creating and using custom stamps in Adobe Acrobat allows you to add personalized annotations, signatures, or symbols to your PDF documents. Stamps are useful for indicating approval, signing documents, or providing feedback. The steps belwo can guide you:

Creating a Custom Stamp:

- Launch Adobe Acrobat on your computer.
- Open the PDF document to which you want to add a custom stamp.
- Click on the "Tools" tab in the upper-left corner to open the Tools pane. In the Tools pane, locate and click on the "Comment" tool to reveal the commenting tools.
- Within the commenting tools, find and click on the "Stamp" tool. This will open a menu with pre-defined stamps.
- Click on the small triangle next to the stamp icon and choose "Create Custom Stamp" from the drop-down menu.
- In the "Create Custom Stamp" dialog, click on the "Browse" or "Select Image" button. Choose an image file (JPEG, PNG, GIF) or a PDF file that you want to use as your custom stamp.

- Adjust the settings, such as the name of the stamp, the category it belongs to, and the scaling options.
- Click "OK" to save your custom stamp. The new stamp will now be available in the stamp menu under the "Custom" category.

Using custom stamps:

- Click on the "Tools" tab, go to the "Comment" tool, and select the "Stamp" tool.
- In the stamp menu, find the "Custom" category. Your newly created custom stamp should be listed there. Click on it to select it.
- Click on the location in the document where you want to place the stamp. You can click and drag to resize the stamp if necessary.
- Right-click on the stamp to access properties. This allows you to adjust properties such as opacity, rotation, and appearance.

Designing and using custom stamps

This feature allows you to personalize your documents with unique annotations, symbols, or signatures. Custom stamps are useful for indicating approval, adding company logos, or providing feedback. Follow the steps below:

Designing a custom stamp:

- Launch Adobe Acrobat on your computer.
- Open the PDF document to which you want to add a custom stamp.
- Click on the "Tools" tab in the upper-left corner to open the Tools pane. In the Tools pane, locate and click on the "Comment" tool to reveal the commenting tools.
- Within the commenting tools, find and click on the "Stamp" tool. This will open a menu with pre-defined stamps.
- Click on the small triangle next to the stamp icon and choose "Create Custom Stamp" from the drop-down menu.
- In the "Create Custom Stamp" dialog, click on the "Browse" or "Select Image" button. Choose an image file (JPEG, PNG, GIF) or a PDF file that you want to use as your custom stamp.
- Adjust the settings, such as the name of the stamp, the category it belongs to, and the scaling options.
- Click "OK" to save your custom stamp. The new stamp will now be available in the stamp menu under the "Custom" category.

Designing a custom stamp image:

- Design your custom stamp using graphic design software like Adobe Photoshop or Illustrator. Ensure the image has a transparent background for better integration with documents.
- Consider the size and proportions of the image. Adobe Acrobat allows you to scale the stamp when creating it, but it's helpful to have an appropriately sized image to start with.

- Save your design as an image (JPEG, PNG, GIF) or as a PDF file if your design includes vector graphics or text. PDF files provide better quality for vector-based designs.

Adding metadata to custom stamps

Metadata in PDF documents refers to information such as title, author, subject, and keywords, and this information is usually managed through the document properties. However, you can include additional information within the stamp itself or leverage existing features to associate metadata-like information with custom stamps by following the tips below:

Option 1: Include information in the stamp image

- When creating the custom stamp image, you can include relevant information directly within the image itself. This could be text, symbols, or any other visual elements that convey metadata.
- If your stamp includes text or other elements that benefit from vector quality, consider saving it as a PDF rather than an image file. This ensures better quality when scaling.

Option 2: Use custom stamp properties

- After placing a stamp on the document, you can right-click on the stamp and choose "Properties." Here you can add a title and subject to the stamp. While this information won't be traditional metadata, it can serve as a way to associate information with the stamp.
- If you are comfortable with JavaScript, you might explore using JavaScript actions within the stamp. JavaScript can be used to perform various actions, and you could potentially use it to associate additional data. This, however, requires scripting knowledge.

Option 3: Use comments and annotations

- Instead of a traditional stamp, you can use text annotations to add information directly to the document. Text annotations allow you to add comments and information that can be associated with specific points on the document.
- When adding comments or annotations, you can use the "Properties" options to add custom fields or information. This could serve as a workaround to associate metadata-like information with your annotations.

Chapter 17

Importing PDFs into InDesign, Illustrator, etc.

Best practices for importing PDFs into Creative Cloud apps

Importing PDFs into Creative Cloud apps is a common workflow, especially when you want to work with existing content in applications like Adobe Illustrator, Adobe Photoshop, or Adobe InDesign. Check below fpr some best practices to consider when importing PDFs into Creative Cloud apps:

Understand the PDF content: Before importing, review the content of the PDF. Understand the structure, layers, and resolution of images within the PDF. This helps you make informed decisions during the import process.

Choose the right application: Select the appropriate Creative Cloud application based on your task. For example, use Adobe Illustrator for vector graphics, Adobe Photoshop for raster images, and Adobe InDesign for layout and multi-page documents.

Vector vs. raster graphics: Consider the nature of the graphics in the PDF. If the content is primarily vector-based, Illustrator is a good choice. If it involves high-resolution images, Photoshop may be more suitable.

Preserve editability: If you need to edit the individual elements of the PDF, choose import options that preserve editability. Illustrator, for instance, allows you to import PDFs with editable text and vector graphics.

Resolution settings: When importing into Photoshop, pay attention to resolution settings, especially if you plan to print the final document. Adjust the resolution to match your intended output.

Editing and updating linked PDFs

This feature involves managing linked files in your document, making changes to the source files, and updating the links to reflect those changes. Check below for steps on how to edit and update linked PDFs in Adobe Acrobat:

- Launch Adobe Acrobat and open the PDF document that contains linked files.
- In Adobe Acrobat, go to the "View" menu and select "Show/Hide" > "Navigation Panes" > "Attachments." This displays the Attachments panel, which shows linked files.
- In the Attachments panel, you'll see a list of linked files associated with the PDF document. Identify the files you want to edit and update.
- Locate and edit the source files of the linked PDFs using the appropriate software. For example, if the linked file is an image, use an image editing tool. If it's another PDF, open and edit it in Adobe Acrobat or another PDF editing application.
- Save the changes you made to the source files. This is a crucial step because updating linked files involves reflecting the changes made in the source files within the PDF document.

- Go back to Adobe Acrobat, and in the Attachments panel, right-click on the linked file you edited. Select "Update" or "Replace" from the context menu. This prompts Acrobat to refresh the link and apply the changes from the source file.
- Adobe Acrobat may prompt you to confirm the update. Confirm the update to replace the existing linked file with the edited version.
- Review the entire PDF document to ensure that the changes made to the linked files are reflected correctly. Pay attention to any annotations, comments, or other elements that may be affected by the updates.

Collaborating with Adobe Document Cloud

Adobe Document Cloud offers features that enhance collaboration and streamline workflows. Learn below how to collaborate using Adobe Document Cloud in Adobe Acrobat:

- To access Adobe Document Cloud services, you need an Adobe ID. Create one if you don't have it, or sign in with your existing Adobe ID.
- Launch Adobe Acrobat and open the PDF document you want to collaborate on.
- In Adobe Acrobat, click on the "Share" button in the upper-right corner. This opens the Share pane.
- Choose how you want to share the document. Options may include email, link sharing, or sending for review. Select the appropriate option based on your collaboration needs.
- If you choose email sharing, enter the email addresses of the collaborators, set permissions (view, comment, edit), and add a message. Collaborators will receive an email invitation.
- If you choose link sharing, generate a shareable link and set permissions. You can copy and share this link with collaborators via email, messaging apps, or other communication channels.
- If you choose to send for review, you can send the document to others for feedback. Enter email addresses, set review deadlines, and customize review settings.
- Collaborators can open the shared document in their Adobe Acrobat or Adobe Reader. Edits and comments are synced in real-time, allowing for seamless collaboration.
- Collaborators can add comments, annotations, and markups to the document. Use the Comments pane to view and respond to comments.

Overview of Adobe Document Cloud services

Adobe Document Cloud is a comprehensive suite of cloud-based services and applications designed to streamline document management, enhance collaboration, and simplify workflows. It offers a range of tools that allow users to create, edit, share, sign, and manage PDF documents across various devices. check below for the key services within Adobe Document Cloud:

Adobe Acrobat DC: Adobe Acrobat DC is the central application within Adobe Document Cloud, providing a powerful set of tools for working with PDF documents. It allows users to create, edit, convert, sign, and share PDFs.

Adobe Sign: Adobe Sign is Adobe's electronic signature solution, formerly known as EchoSign. It enables users to send, sign, track, and manage digital documents securely. Adobe Sign is integrated into Adobe Acrobat and other applications for a seamless signing experience.

Adobe Scan: Adobe Scan is a mobile application that turns your smartphone or tablet into a portable scanner. It allows users to capture, enhance, and save documents, receipts, business cards, and whiteboards as high-quality PDFs.

Adobe Fill & Sign: Adobe Fill & Sign is a mobile and web application that simplifies the process of filling out and signing forms. Users can fill, sign, and send forms without the need for printing and scanning.

Adobe PDF Pack: It is a subscription service that provides online PDF conversion. Users can convert various file formats, including Word, Excel, and PowerPoint, into PDFs. It also allows the export of PDFs to editable formats.

Adobe Export PDF: Adobe Export PDF is a service that enables users to convert PDFs into editable Word or Excel documents. It facilitates extracting content from PDFs for further editing.

Adobe Document Cloud for teams and enterprise: Adobe offers Document Cloud plans tailored for teams and enterprises. These plans provide advanced collaboration features, enhanced security controls, and centralized administration for managing users and access.

Collaborative features and benefits

Adobe Acrobat offers a variety of collaborative features and benefits that empower users to work together on PDF documents efficiently. Whether you're reviewing, commenting, or collecting feedback, these features enhance collaboration and streamline document workflows. Check below for collaborative features and their associated benefits in Adobe Acrobat:

Commenting and Markup: Users can add comments, annotations, and markups directly on PDF documents. It facilitates collaboration by allowing users to provide feedback, suggestions, and corrections; it equally enables communication and discussion within the document itself.

Real-time collaboration: Multiple users can collaborate on a PDF document in real time. it enhances teamwork by allowing users to work simultaneously on a document. It also offers real-time updates, which ensure everyone is on the same page during collaborative sessions.

Shared reviews: Users can initiate shared reviews, sending the document to others for feedback. **It** simplifies the review process by collecting feedback from multiple collaborators. It equally allows for a structured and organized review with tracking and commenting features.

Review tracker:

Provides a summary view of comments, annotations, and changes made during a review. It streamlines the review process by offering an overview of all feedback and helps document owners manage and address comments effectively.

Integration with Adobe Sign: Adobe Acrobat integrates with Adobe Sign for electronic signatures. **It** enables secure and legally binding electronic signatures on PDF documents. In addition, it streamlines approval processes and document signing workflows.

Form collaboration:

Supports collaboration on forms, allowing multiple users to fill out and submit forms electronically. It helps to eliminate the need for physical paperwork by enabling digital form completion. It also enhances efficiency in collecting and processing form data.

Access control and permissions: Document owners can set access permissions, restricting or allowing specific actions for collaborators. **It** ensures document security by controlling who can view, edit, comment, or print the document, and provides flexibility in managing collaborative workflows.

www.ingramcontent.com/pod-product-compliance
Lightning Source LLC
La Vergne TN
LVHW081529050326
832903LV00025B/1702